EYEWITNESS

TOP

VANCOUVER
& VANCOUVER ISLAND

CONSTANCE BRISSENDEN

DK | Penguin Random House

Top 10 Vancouver and Vancouver Island Highlights

The Top 10 of Everything

CONTENTS

Vancouver and Vancouver Island Area by Area

Streetsmart

Within each Top 10 list in this book, no hierarchy of quality or popularity is implied. All ten are, in the editor's opinion, of roughly equal merit.
  Throughout this book, floors are referred to in accordance with American usage: i.e., the "first floor" is at ground level.

Front cover and spine *Vancouver skyline in front of North Shore Mountains*
Back cover *Panoramic view of Tofino on the West coast of Vancouver Island.*
Title page *The famous Totem Poles at Capilano Suspension Bridge Park, Vancouver.*

Welcome to
Vancouver and Vancouver Island

A city of gleaming skyscrapers surrounded by ocean and stunning mountain scenery, Vancouver has world-class art galleries and museums, stunning green spaces, and a food scene to get excited about. A short journey away, Vancouver Island offers spectacular scenery. With Eyewitness Top 10 Vancouver and Vancouver Island, the area is yours to explore.

The Waterfront and Downtown districts are likely to be your first introduction to the city; some outstanding attractions nestle near glitzy **Canada Place**, including **Christ Church Cathedral**, **Vancouver Art Gallery**, **Vancouver Lookout**, and **Science World**. A 14-mile (22-km) waterfront greenway meanders around the edges of **Stanley Park**, a rare urban wilderness with incredible vistas. Hop over by ferry to the south shore, where sprawling **Vanier Park** is home to the **H. R. MacMillan Space Centre** and a collection of museums, or explore **Granville Island** and its bustling Public Market.

Beyond the city, Greater Vancouver boasts **Capilano Suspension Bridge Park**, plus a mind-blowing array of outdoor pursuits in Whistler. With its wild coastline, **Vancouver Island** is also a popular outdoor destination. Its laid-back provincial capital **Victoria** is home to the **Royal British Columbia Museum** and historic **Inner Harbour**.

Whether you're visiting for a weekend or a week, our Top 10 guide brings together the best of everything Vancouver and Vancouver Island has to offer, from the trendiest restaurants to a year-round roster of festivals and events. The guide has useful tips throughout, from seeking out what's free to avoiding the crowds, plus seven easy-to-follow itineraries designed to tie together a clutch of sights in a short space of time. Add inspiring photography and detailed maps, and you've got the essential pocket-sized travel companion. **Enjoy the book, and enjoy Vancouver and Vancouver Island.**

Clockwise from top: **Detail of the sails at Canada Place; British Columbia Parliament Buildings, Victoria; Capilano Suspension Bridge, Greater Vancouver; Vancouver skyscrapers; totem pole in Stanley Park; ski slopes in Whistler; sunken garden in Butchart Gardens, Victoria**

Exploring Vancouver and Vancouver Island

The city of Vancouver – buzzing with culture and a fabulous food scene – is surrounded by ocean, mountains and old-growth forest, with stunning Vancouver Island just across the Georgia Strait. Here are a few ideas for your stay, whether you only have time for the must-see sights, or can explore Greater Vancouver and beyond.

The striking sail-like silhouette of Canada Place, built for Expo '86, is instantly recognizable.

Key
— Two-day itinerary
— Seven-day itinerary

Two Days in Vancouver

Day ❶
MORNING
Take a stroll around **Canada Place** *(see pp14–15)* to view the harbor. Jump on the SkyTrain at landmark Waterfront Station to explore the award-winning **Science World** *(see pp26–7)*. Afterwards, eat lunch in hip **Gastown** *(see p69)*.

AFTERNOON
Check out either the much-loved **Vancouver Art Gallery** *(see pp20–21)* or the captivating **Bill Reid Gallery** *(see p77)*, then window-shop on bustling **Robson Street** *(see p76)*. Afterwards, treat yourself to dinner or cocktails at one of the swanky downtown eateries *(see p81)*.

Day ❷
MORNING
Hire a bike to explore the green lungs of the city, **Stanley Park** *(see pp12–13)*, and visit its mind-blowing Aquarium *(see p13)*. Follow the Seawall as it snakes around the edge of the park to take in views of Burrard Inlet and English Bay, and then ride the Aquabus to **Granville Island** *(see pp24–5)*.

AFTERNOON
Delight in the local produce and hand-made wares at **Granville Island Public Market** *(see p86)* and, if you have the energy, cycle on to the museums in **Vanier Park** *(see p85)*, or head to **Sunset Beach** *(see p83)*.

Granville Island Public Market sells an enticing array of fresh local produce.

Sublime mountain scenery can be found in Whistler, just a short drive from Vancouver.

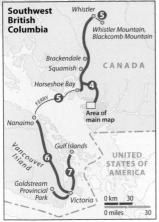

Seven Days in Vancouver and Vancouver Island

Days ❶ and ❷
Follow the activities in the two-day Vancouver itinerary.

Day ❸
Take the SeaBus from Waterfront Station to Lonsdale Quay and its market in **North Vancouver** *(see p102)*. Don't miss the West Coast rain forest and the dizzying views from the **Capilano Suspension Bridge** *(see pp16–17)*. Afterwards, return to the city, where 20 minutes from downtown, Northwest Coast First Nations art and culture is celebrated at the unparalleled **Museum of Anthropology at UBC** *(see pp18–19)*. Combine your visit with a walking tour of the campus.

Day ❹
Set off on the 75-mile (120-km) drive to **Whistler** *(see pp34–5)* on the Sea-to-Sky Highway (Hwy 99), taking in adventure-sports paradise **Squamish** *(see p102)* and the small town of **Brackendale** *(see p103)* en route.

Day ❺
Explore Whistler Village and ride the gondola up Whistler Mountain where you'll find hiking trails and the PEAK 2 PEAK gondola to Blackcomb Mountain for superb alpine sightseeing. Drive to Horseshoe Bay in West Vancouver for the ferry to **Nanaimo** *(see p94)*.

Day ❻
After exploring Nanaimo's Old Quarter, make a beeline to provincial capital **Victoria** *(see pp28–9)*. Here, take in the city's Inner Harbour and the outstanding **Royal British Columbia Museum** *(see pp30–31)*.

Day ❼
Dedicate your final day to the great outdoors. Hike in old-growth rain forest at **Goldstream Provincial Park** *(see p94)*, try a whale-watching tour, or head to the **Gulf Islands** *(see p93)*.

Top 10 Vancouver and Vancouver Island Highlights

Canada Place and Vancouver
Waterfront at dusk

TOP10 Vancouver and Vancouver Island Highlights

Poised between the Pacific Ocean and the Coast Mountain range, Vancouver is one of the most beautifully located cities on earth. With a lively cultural scene and great restaurants, it is often listed among the world's best places to live. A short ferry ride away, Victoria is a great base from which to explore the many natural wonders of Vancouver Island.

1 Stanley Park
Created in 1888, Stanley Park is North America's third-largest urban park. It offers a heady mix of forest and ocean (see pp12–13).

2 Canada Place
Built for Expo '86, Canada Place is an outstanding convention and hotel complex overlooking Vancouver Harbour. Cruise ships dock alongside an inviting promenade (see pp14–15).

3 Capilano Suspension Bridge Park
Teeter over a wooden bridge high above the Capilano River, walk along a boardwalk into the treetops, and learn about local history, forest ecology, and First Nations culture at this incredible park (see pp16–17).

4 Museum of Anthropology at UBC
Located n a stunning building is one of North America's finest collections of Northwest Coast First Nations and Inuit art. There is also a great collection of European ceramics (see pp18–19).

5 Vancouver Art Gallery
From the swirling forests of BC artist Emily Carr to radical installations, the gallery features the best of West Coast and international art (see pp20–21).

Around Vancouver

Campbell River • Powell River • Whistler (10)
Gold River • Courtenay • Garibaldi • BRITISH COLUMBIA • Brackendale
Texada Island • Squamish
Port Alberni • Parksville • Sechelt • Horseshoe Bay (3) • Vancouver
Tofino • Nanaimo • Ladysmith • Tsawwassen
Ucluelet • Lake Cowichan • U.S.A.
Bamfield • Honeymoon Bay • Duncan
Clo-oose • Sidney
Port Renfrew • Sooke • Victoria (8)

0 km 50
0 miles 50

(2) Vancouver Harbour

TREET
BURRARD STREET • WEST HASTINGS ST • Portside Park
DUNSMUIR ST • GASTOWN • MAPLE TREE SQUARE
(5) ROBSON SQUARE • VICTORY SQUARE • EAST HASTINGS ST
SMITHE • SEYMOUR STREET • WEST HOMER ST
WEST GEORGIA ST • CHINATOWN • MAIN ST
NELSON STREET • LIBRARY SQUARE • EXPO BLVD
YALETOWN (WAREHOUSE DISTRICT)
PACIFIC • BOULEVARD • Creekside Park
Coopers Park • CAMBIE STREET • (7)
Creek
0 meters 800
0 yards 800

6 Granville Island

This popular island on False Creek is a bustling mix of shops, galleries, restaurants, and theaters (see pp24–5).

7 Science World

Science comes alive inside the dome-shaped Science World. Hands-on exhibits inspire and capture the imaginations of all ages (see pp26–7).

8 Victoria

With its historic buildings and green parks, Victoria makes a great base for trips around Vancouver Island (see pp28–9).

9 Around Long Beach

Wild Pacific shores, rare old-growth forests and spectacular scenery abound in the Long Beach area on Vancouver Island's rugged west coast (see pp32–3).

Whistler 10

Ideally placed for a city escape, Whistler is an upscale resort a two-hour drive north from Vancouver. Two mountains tower over alpine-style resort villages. Skiers abound here but there are countless other year-round activities (see pp34–5).

TOP 10 ⭐ Stanley Park

A local favorite since the Victorian era, spectacular Stanley Park is a mere ten-minute bus ride from downtown. Forest walks, beachside strolls, and a vibrant rose garden are among its natural attractions. Activities include a popular children's water park, playgrounds, tennis courts, and a pitch-and-putt course. Located in the park, the Vancouver Aquarium is world-renowned for its realistic walk-through exhibits based on scientific research projects.

1 Lost Lagoon

This willow-fringed lagoon **(above)** is a wild-life sanctuary. It protects a bevy of wood ducks, blue herons, and white swans.

2 Siwash Rock

According to Squamish legend, this ancient lava rock deposit jutting up from the water was once an Indian warrior, turned to stone.

4 Rose Garden

A formal rose garden blossoms year-round. From April to September, a variety of perennial plantings ensure vibrant color.

THE HISTORY OF STANLEY PARK

Home to First Nations tribes for thousands of years before Europeans arrived, the peninsula was used by colonialists as a military reserve because of its strategic position. In 1888 it was established as a city park, dedicated to Governor General Stanley. To stop erosion, the Seawall was constructed in 1917.

3 Seawall

Pedestrians, cyclists, and in-line skaters happily share the 6-mile (10-km) paved path ringing the park **(below)**, with its unimpeded views of English Bay and Burrard Inlet. Look out for the sculpture *Girl in a Wetsuit* on an offshore rock.

Prospect Point ⑤

Set on the northern tip of the peninsula, just west of the Lions Gate Bridge, this is the park's highest point. The view from here **(right)**, across the dark-blue water of Burrard Inlet to the Coast Mountains, is one of the best in the city.

⑥ Brockton Point Visitor Centre

Carved gateways and a cedarwood interpretive pavilion welcome visitors. One of the poles on display is a copy of a pre-1878 Skedans mortuary pole carved by Haida artist Bill Reid.

⑨ Brockton Point

The point offers a terrific view of Burrard Inlet. In 1915, a lighthouse was built to guide vessels into the harbor. Sailors set their chronometers by the Nine-O'Clock Gun at nearby Hallelujah Point. Its boom has been heard nightly since 1894.

⑩ Vancouver Aquarium

Marine displays capture the drama of the West Coast. Sharks, rays, penguins, jellyfish **(below)** and lots of other sea creatures from around the globe can be seen here.

Stanley Park

⑦ English Bay

The sandy beaches at the bay draw crowds. Sunbathers relax against driftwood logs at Third Beach, and the heated saltwater pool at Second Beach offers a warmer alternative to the bay.

⑧ Beaver Lake

Hiking trails to Beaver Lake follow old logging roads through a raincoast forest. Frogs, raccoons, and rabbits may be spotted at the natural-state lake fringed by cattails and water lilies.

NEED TO KNOW

MAP G1 ▪ 311 ▪ www. vancouver.ca

Main Park: open 24 hrs daily (washrooms open dawn–dusk)

Vancouver Aquarium: 845 Avison Way; 604 659 3474; open late Jun–Aug: 9:30am–7pm, Sep–mid-Jun:

10am–5pm; adm adult $39, seniors, youths & students $30, kids $22, under-3s free; www.vanaqua.org

▪ Numerous concession stands, cafés, and food trucks can be found throughout the park. The Aquarium's two cafés offer breakfast and lunch options.

▪ Traffic in the park is one way (counterclockwise) and parking fees are strictly enforced.

▪ Rent a bicycle or in-line skates to cover more of the park. Bayshore Rentals (745 Denman St; 604 688 2453; www.bayshorebike rentals.ca) is a good hire company nearby.

TOP 10 ⭐ Canada Place

Built for Expo '86 as the flagship Canada Pavilion, Canada Place is a Vancouver landmark. The roof's futuristic sail-like lines echo Canada's nautical roots. The "prow" extends well into the harbor. Following the highly successful world exhibition, which attracted more than 22 million visitors, Canada Place was transformed into a complex containing a cruise-ship terminal, a convention center, exhibition areas, and a first-class hotel. The promenade offers a terrific view of the city's harbor.

1 Architecture
Built for Expo '86 on the site of a former cargo dock, Canada Place's award-winning design is notable for its five Teflon-coated fiberglass sails, resembling a sailing ship **(above)**.

2 Tourism Vancouver Visitor Centre
Operated by Tourism Vancouver, this useful bureau, located across Canada Place, offers free brochures and city maps. The volunteer staff are knowledgeable and multilingual.

3 The Canadian Trail
The trail **(below)** is a walk through Canadian history. Interactive exhibits high-light Canada's heritage, innovations, sports, and geography. The walkway also offers great views of Stanley Park and the North Shore Mountains.

4 Vancouver Convention Centre
This state-of-the-art, eco-designed facility **(above)** has a landscaped, gray-water-irrigated "living roof," the largest in Canada, and is home to 60,000 honey bees as well as nearly half a million native plants.

7 Community Events

Canada Place hosts a variety of events, ranging from free yoga classes and busker performances in summer to Canada Day celebrations with fireworks on July 1 **(left)**.

5 Port Metro Vancouver's Discovery Centre

Located at the north end of Canada Place, this center educates visitors about the port through interactive touchscreen kiosks, videos, and presentations.

EXPO '86

On May 2, 1986, Prince Charles and Princess Diana opened Expo '86, a hugely successful international fair. It unfortunately closed with a $311-million deficit. However, the enduring legacies, such as Canada Place, Science World, the SkyTrain, and the urban renewal of False Creek, show that Expo '86 ultimately gave back a great deal to the people of Vancouver.

9 Cruise Ship Terminal

A three-berth cruise ship terminal is adjacent to the promenade at Canada Place, and welcomes hundreds of thousands of visitors a year. From the terminal, it's a short walk to the sights and shops of Gastown *(see p69)*.

6 Heritage Horns

Every day, at noon, the sound of ten air horns blasts across Vancouver from the top of Canada Place. Designed and built by Robert Swanson in 1967 as a project to celebrate Canada's 100th birthday, the first four notes of the chimes are from the national anthem, *O Canada*.

8 Floatplanes

Pontooned planes **(above)** from Victoria land at Coal Harbour, west of Canada Place. Helicopters from Victoria descend to the east of the complex.

NEED TO KNOW

MAP L2 ▪ 999 Canada Pl ▪ 604 665 9000 ▪ www.canadaplace.ca

Tourism Vancouver Visitor Centre: 200 Burrard St; 604 682 2222; open 9am–5pm daily; www.tourismvancouver.com

FlyOver™ Canada: 201-999 Canada Pl; 604 620 8455; open 10am–9pm; adm; www.flyovercanada.com

▪ Underground paid parking is available at Canada Place. Less pricey parking can be found in the lot at the north end of Burrard Street.

10 FlyOver™ Canada

Visitors of all ages can soar from coast to coast on a breathtaking virtual journey that takes in the excitement and grandeur of Canada's landscape in the latest flight ride technology. Wind, sounds, and scents all add to the experience.

TOP 10 ★ Capilano Suspension Bridge Park

For thrill appeal, few sites rival Capilano Suspension Bridge Park. The park's star attraction is the marvelous suspension footbridge that sways 230 ft (70 m) above the gushing Capilano River. Visitors can also get a squirrel's-eye perspective of the West Coast rainforest that lies along treetop bridges, or walk across a spectacular cliffside walkway straddling the deep Capilano Canyon. This remarkable park is one of Vancouver's most popular attractions.

Suspension Bridge ①

This awe-inspiring bridge is built of steel cables spanning 450 ft (137 m) and strong enough to support a full Boeing 747. Those crossing the bridge **(right)** cling to the handrails as they experience the same thrills visitors did in 1889.

② The Kia'palano Big House

Set at the center of the Kia'palano Big House is the Next Generation story pole, honoring First Nations artists. An interactive exhibit with a First Nations interpreter is in the open-fronted Little Big House (a smaller version of the Big House).

③ Treetops Adventure

This exhilarating exhibit leads you gently upwards over seven suspension bridges attached to eight old-growth Douglas fir trees **(left)**. At the end of your journey, you are 100 ft (30 m) high in the mid-story treetops.

④ Treetops Technology

Treetops Adventure uses an innovative compression system to secure observation platforms to the trees. Instead of nails or screws, friction collars are used. Held on by compression, they exert a gentle pressure.

⑤ Cliffwalk

Almost 700 ft (213 m) of bridges and stairs **(above)** lead along the cliff edge, offering stunning views of the Capilano River gorge 230 ft (70 m) below.

⑥ English Country Garden

This perennial garden harks back to the homeland of many of Vancouver's early settlers. Planted in 1910, the azaleas and rhododendrons dazzle with colorful blooms. The garden is at its best in May.

⑦ Totem Poles

At the centre's entrance, totem poles carved by local Coast Salish First Nations people make a colorful display **(right)**. Introduced in the 1930s, the poles now number more than 30.

⑧ Locals from the Past

Friendly costumed guides in period attire welcome visitors to the park. Taking on the roles of local historical characters, the guides narrate the often hair-raising stories of the North Shore's early days, when timber was king.

⑨ Living Forest

Clever interactive displays educate visitors about native plants and trees. Panels feature the animals and bugs living in a West Coast rain forest, and naturalists offer guided tours on its peaceful forest trails.

A LASTING LEGACY

Scotsman George Grant MacKay loved the outdoors. As Vancouver's first park commissioner, he voted for Stanley Park in 1886. Two years later, he bought 9 sq miles (23 sq km) of old-growth forest along the Capilano River and built a cabin on the edge of the canyon wall. With the help of local Coast Salish people, he built a hemp rope and cedar suspension bridge in 1889. This was the very first bridge.

⑩ Story Centre

From miners to loggers to dancehall girls, the centre **(below)** tells the history of the park and of wider North Vancouver in a walk-through exhibit. Hundreds of captioned photographs bring history to life. Voices from the Past, an audio component, fills in any blanks.

NEED TO KNOW

MAP B1 ▪ 3735 Capilano Rd, North Vancouver ▪ 604 985 7474 ▪ www.capbridge.com

Open Feb–May & Sep–Nov: 9am–dusk, Jun–Aug: 8am–8pm, Dec–Jan: 11am–9pm; closed Dec 25

Adm adults $42.95, seniors $38.95, students $33.95, youth (13–16) $26.95, children $14.95 (under 6s free)

▪ The Logger's Grill at the park serves juicy beef and salmon burgers while the various cafés on-site offer coffee and snacks. The free shuttle service picks up park visitors from four downtown locations.

▪ If heights are a concern when crossing the bridge, focus on the back of the person in front. It's worth making the trip across.

TOP 10 ⭐ Museum of Anthropology at UBC

Founded in 1947 and located in a breathtaking setting at the University of British Columbia (UBC), this museum houses one of the world's finest displays of Northwest Coast First Nations art. Here you'll also find European ceramics, Asian textiles, Greek and Roman pottery, and African masks, as well as many full-size totem poles and contemporary carvings. The magnificent building, designed by Canadian architect Arthur Erickson, is a historic work of art inspired by the post-and-beam structures of northern Northwest Coast First Nations.

1 Welcome Figure

On the museum's outdoor welcome plaza stands a red cedar welcome figure holding a *fisher* (an animal believed to have healing powers). It was created by Musqueam artist Susan Point.

2 Bentwood Boxes

These boxes **(above)**, used for cooking as well as storage, are made in a very special way. The four sides are composed of one piece of cedar, which is steamed and bent to form the shape of the box before the base is added.

3 Haida Houses

Two full-size Haida Houses **(above)** stand outside, surrounded by a forest of soaring, full-scale totem poles. They were designed in 1962 by contemporary Haida artist Bill Reid and Namgis artist Doug Cramer.

4 Totem Poles

Beneath the 49-ft (15-m) glass walls of the Great Hall are show-cased towering totem poles **(below)** from many First Nations. The glass and concrete structure of the hall provides a perfect setting for the poles.

5 The Raven and the First Men

This massive sculpture **(right)**, by Bill Reid, is one of the most famous carvings in the world. It shows the figure of Raven (a wise yet mischievous trickster) discovering the first Haida humans and coaxing them out into the world from a giant clamshell.

GOING DEEP UNDERGROUND

The museum is built on three World War II gun emplacements, which were incorporated into the design of the building. Two are located outside the grounds, one of which is the platform for Bill Reid's *Raven*. A maze of secret tunnels connects the bunkers under the building.

7 Athenian Black Band Cup

Housed in the classical pottery collection, this cup was made in Greece in 540–530 BC. It is attributed to the "Centaur Painter," one of a group of artists known for decorating drinking cups used by men in Athens at famous symposia or loud drinking parties.

9 Carved Doors

These massive doors were carved from red cedar in 1976 by Gitxsan artists from the 'Ksan Historical Village (see p42). They tell the story of the first people of the Skeena River region in British Columbia.

8 Ceramic Stove

The centerpiece of the Koerner Ceramics Gallery is a stove from Central or Eastern Europe, around 1500–1600. Its lead-glazed tiles depict popular religious figures of the time.

10 Weaving

Weaving has always been important for Salish people – woven objects from 4,500 years ago have been excavated at Musqueam. This display revitalizes and pays homage to this tradition.

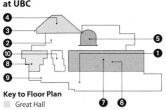

Museum of Anthropology at UBC

- ❹
- ❸
- ❷
- ❿
- ❽
- ❾
- ❺
- ❶

Key to Floor Plan

- ▨ Great Hall
- ▨ Bill Reid Rotunda
- ▨ Koerner European Ceramic Gallery
- ▨ Multiversity Galleries

❼ ❻

6 New Guinea Necklaces

These ornate necklaces form part of the museum's founding collection of South Pacific materials, donated in 1927 by Canadian explorer Frank Burnett.

NEED TO KNOW

MAP A2 ■ 6393 NW Marine Dr ■ 604 822 5087 ■ www.moa.ubc.ca

Open 10am–5pm daily (to 9pm Thu); closed on Mon in winter

Adm adults $18, senior/students $16, under-6s free, flat fee 5–9pm Thu $10

■ The museum shop is renowned for its outstanding selection of original gold and silver jewelry, prints, argillite, textiles, and other treasures.

■ Parking is available at the Rose Garden Parkade, opposite the museum

■ The museum café sells a good selection of sandwiches and drinks.

TOP 10 ★ Vancouver Art Gallery

The Vancouver Art Gallery is the largest art gallery in Western Canada. With the most significant collection of works by Emily Carr, BC's preeminent artist and writer, it is well worth the entry fee. The gallery specializes in impressive national and international exhibitions, with innovative approaches to old masters as well as contemporary visionaries. The gallery's collection comprises more than 10,000 works, including a large collection of photo-based art by Vancouver's international art superstar Jeff Wall and renowned Haida artist Robert Davidson. Housed in a Neo-Classical heritage building redesigned by acclaimed local architect Arthur Erickson, the gallery opened in 1983.

EMILY CARR

Although Emily Carr was born into a very wealthy Victoria family in 1871, the eccentric artist chose a bohemian lifestyle instead, painting on a pauper's budget, often in the old-growth forests of Haida Gwaii (Queen Charlotte Islands). It was only in 1937 that the Vancouver Art Gallery bought one of her works. Largely overlooked during her lifetime, Carr's works now command some of the highest prices in Canada.

② First Nations Art

Paintings, carvings, and sculpture by Pacific Northwest First Nations artists are part of the gallery's rotating permanent collection, which includes sculptures by late Haida master carver Bill Reid. Reflecting the Modernist style of many First Nations artists, *Eagles* **(below)**, by Haida artist Robert Davidson, combines principles of abstraction with traditional First Nations iconography.

① Court House Building

Built in 1912 as the Provincial Court House, the building reflects the imposing style of the era's leading Canadian architect, Francis Rattenbury.

③ Architecture

Architectural icon Arthur Erickson added 41,400 sq ft (3,715 sq m) of exhibition space to the old Provincial Court House when transforming it into the gallery's home **(below)**. Erickson kept many of the original features, including the courtroom, with its carved judge's bench.

④ Exhibitions Program

The celebrated works of Monet, Picasso, Botticelli, Cézanne, the Dutch masters, and the Group of Seven are just a sample of the recent exhibitions shown at the VAG. Works of local and emerging talents from around the globe are also exhibited.

⑤ Art on the Rooftop

Vancouver artist Ken Lum's innovative *Four Boats Stranded: Red and Yellow, Black and White* stands out on the gallery's roof. The installation includes a scaled-down version of a First Nations longboat.

7 Jeff Wall Collection

Local artist Jeff Wall's photographic works, presented in large light boxes, focus on complex urban environments and feature images inspired by social issues.

8 Southern Façade

Overlooking Robson Street, the original steps into the court house are a popular meeting spot for locals. On the portico **(below)** is the work *Placed Upon the Horizon (Casting Shadows)* by conceptual artist Lawrence Weiner. The letters here were carved in yellow cedar.

6 Emily Carr Collection

The Gallery holds more than 200 works by Emily Carr. This renowned West Coast artist studied local First Nations cultures, capturing their way of life in her paintings. Haida artifacts such as totem poles were a common subject. Stormy West Coast colors as seen, for example, in *Totem Poles, Kitseukla* **(above)**, dominate her work. Items such as her tiny sketchbook are also on display.

NEED TO KNOW

MAP K3 ▪ 750 Hornby St ▪ 604 662 4719 ▪ www.vanartgallery.bc.ca

Open 10am–5pm daily (to 9pm Tue)

Adm adult $24, $20, students $18, children $6.50, under-5s and gallery members free, by donation 5–9pm Tue

▪ The Gallery Café patio *(see p80)* is lovely on sunny days. You do not need to pay admission to the gallery to eat at the café.

▪ The Gallery Store sells contemporary art books, posters, paper goods, jewelry and giftware, including a wide range of Emily Carr merchandise.

9 Photoconceptual Collection

The gallery is known for its permanent collection of contemporary photo-based art. It spans two decades and includes works by the Vancouver School of artists, such as Jeff Wall, Stan Douglas, Ian Wallace, and Ken Lum, as well as famous international artists Nancy Spero and Cindy Sherman, among others.

10 Family Programming

The gallery makes art accessible to younger visitors with family-focused activities every Saturday and every other Sunday, as well as three "mega" family-oriented weekends each year. There are also regular events for teenagers.

Following pages Science World lit up at night

TOP 10 ⭐ Granville Island

Bustling Granville Island attracts millions of visitors every year, and rightly so. Where heavy industries once belched noxious fumes, street entertainers now amuse passersby with music, comedy, and magic. The Granville Island Public Market offers an enchanting mix of edibles and collectibles. More than 200 shops scattered throughout the Island sell everything from custom-made jewelry to yachts.

③ Net Loft

This intimate collection of boutiques sells unusual souvenirs, such as handmade paper, hats, offbeat postcards, beads of all kinds, and local and First Nations crafts.

④ Arts Club Theatre and Lounge

The Arts Club Theatre Company produces contemporary comedies and classics at the Granville Island Stage. The casual Backstage Lounge *(see p88)* showcases local bands.

(see p88)

① Kids Market

Fun is guaranteed in this fantasyland for kids **(above)**. More than 20 shops sell everything from games and toys to pint-sized clothing.

② Marina and Maritime Market

Shops and services at the market include seafood merchants, tours, boat rentals, and marine souvenir shops. At the marina **(below)**, yachts and sailboats are moored beside rustic fishing boats.

NEED TO KNOW

MAP H5 ■ www.granvilleisland.com

Public Market: open 9am–7pm daily; closed Dec 25 & 26, Jan 1, Mon in Jan

Net Loft and Kids Market: open 10am–7pm daily, Jan–Mar: 10am–6pm

Arts Club Theatre and Lounge: 1585 Johnston St; www.artsclub.com

Marina and Maritime Market: open 8am–4:30pm Mon–Fri

Edible Canada: www.ediblecanada.com

New-Small and Sterling Studio Glass: 1440 Old Bridge St; open 10am–6pm Mon–Sat & 11am–5pm Sun

Granville Island Brewing: 1441 Cartwright St; open noon–9pm daily

Crafthouse: 1386 Cartwright St; open 10am–6pm daily

7 Granville Island Public Market

The public market **(left)** is best known for its irresistible emporium of green grocers, butchers, bakers, fishmongers, importers, stalls selling ethnic foods, craft vendors, sweet stands, florists, and casual eateries *(see p86)*.

5 Edible Canada

Here you'll find the best of what Canadian producers have to offer, from specialist cheeses to locally distilled sake and many other artisan food products, all of which make unique gifts. Stop off at the bistro *(see p89)* or book one of the foodie tours of Chinatown or the public market.

8 Granville Island Brewing

Opened in 1984, this microbrewery was Canada's first. Try their delicious beers **(left)**, made with only natural ingredients, at local pubs or in the brewery's taproom after a behind-the-scenes tour, offered through the week at noon, 2pm, 4pm, and 5:30pm *(see p57)*.

GRANVILLE ISLAND FERRIES

The Aquabus and False Creek Ferries fleets provide year-round services around False Creek, with sailings to and from downtown. They are a fun way to travel to Granville Island. Other routes include stops at Science World, Yaletown, and Vanier Park. Mini sunset cruises are also available.

9 Railspur District

The artisan studio-shops in this laneway **(below)** are run by painters, potters, and craftspeople specializing in wood, fabric, leather, glass, and industrial cast-offs.

6 New-Small and Sterling Studio Glass

Watch David New-Small and apprentices as they blow molten glass into beautiful vases, ornaments, jewelry, and dishes using traditional techniques. One of four furnaces keeps 150 lbs (70 kg) of glass molten at 2,000° F (1,100° C) around the clock.

10 Crafthouse

This trendy gallery and shop sells contemporary fine crafts. The pieces are made by both emerging and established artists who are members of the Craft Council of British Columbia (CCBC).

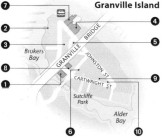

Granville Island

7
2
3
4
5
8
1
9
6
10

Brokers Bay
GRANVILLE BRIDGE
JOHNSTON ST
CARTWRIGHT ST
Sutcliffe Park
Alder Bay

TOP 10 ★ Science World

Fascinating insights into all aspects of the universe are featured at the award-winning Science World at TELUS World of Science. Explorations begin with the smallest insect and progress to the farthest corners of the galaxy. A legacy of Expo '86, the building opened as a science center in 1989. Seven galleries feature hundreds of delightfully interactive, hands-on displays and exhibits based on different themes, as well as entertaining live science demonstrations.

① Feature Gallery

The best traveling exhibitions are showcased here. Always fresh and exciting, the content of the gallery changes every few months. Consistently offering hands-on interactive opportunities for all ages to explore science topics encompassing light, sound, engineering, and more, it's sure to spark your curiosity.

② Wonder Gallery

Designed for kids up to 5 years old, this area has a baby gym, water tables meant for splashing around, a climbing tower, a building blocks zone, and a bus laboratory for fun experiments **(right)**.

③ Geodesic Dome

Science World's 155-ft- (47-m-) tall geodesic dome **(above)** is dubbed "the golf ball" by locals. The design is based on the prototype structure made famous by US inventor and architect R. Buckminster Fuller. Mirror-like exterior panels, 766 in all, reflect the sunlight, while 391 exterior lights sparkle at night.

④ Our World Gallery

This exhibit reveals how the choices we make about waste disposal, food production, and transportation affect our home communities.

⑤ Science Theatre

High-definition films about science, nature, and outer space are shown here. There are cartoons for toddlers and movies for the whole family.

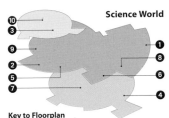

Science World

10
3
9
2
5
7

1
8
6
4

Key to Floorplan
Level 1
Level 2
Level 3

7 Peter Brown Family Centre Stage

Scientific principles and phenomena are explored in five daily shows. Presenters mix balloons and electricity, bubbles and fire to dazzle and captivate.

8 BodyWorks Gallery

This gallery encourages a positive curiosity about the human body. Questions about how human beings hear, smell, and move are answered in this fun-filled interactive space.

Eureka! Gallery 9

Eureka! Gallery **(right)** explores universal themes such as water, air, motion, and invention. Children and adults alike are invited to make their own discoveries in a lifelike science laboratory environment. Use the infrared camera to discover the hot spots on your body.

10 OMNIMAX® Theatre

The five-story screen, one of the largest in the world, envelops viewers with thrilling films. The 400-seat theater, located in the dome, projects images nine times larger than a conventional movie house onto a screen 88 ft (27 m) in diameter.

Search: Sara Stern Gallery 6

Explore natural history with live critters and creepy-crawlies, a replica of a beaver home, a real bee colony, and a life-size Tyrannosaurus rex skeleton cast **(right)**.

NEED TO KNOW

MAP M5 ■ 1455 Quebec St; 604 443 7440

Open summer: 10am–6pm daily; winter: 10am–5pm Mon–Fri, 10am–6pm Sat, Sun & hols; closed Dec 25

Adm adults $23.25, seniors/students/youth (13–18) $18.50, children $15.25, under-3s free; additional fee for OMNIMAX® Theatre

■ White Spot *(see p51)*, a popular BC chain known for its burgers slathered with Triple O (triple oozy) sauce, is on the Science World site. A concession on Level 2 offers juices and ice-cream bars.

■ Paid parking in the small lot is at a premium. Try taking the SkyTrain to Main Street Station, then walking to Science World.

■ Meet the backyard chickens in the fascinating Ken Spencer Science Park located right outside the main center. A diverse range of crops and plants are grown in raised beds here and visitors can learn a lot about recycling through interactive presentations. This part of Science World is open from March to October.

TOP 10 ⭐ Victoria

Picturesque Victoria is the perfect getaway from bustling Vancouver. Established as a fort in 1843 by the Hudson's Bay Company, Victoria became British Columbia (BC)'s capital in 1868, and the growing city attracted top architects such as Francis Mawson Rattenbury. Today the "Garden City" buzzes around the Inner Harbour, and nearby are some excellent museums, the oldest Chinatown in Canada, and the home of Victoria's most famous artist, Emily Carr.

GOVERNOR JAMES DOUGLAS

James Douglas, known as the father of British Columbia, was born in British Guiana (now called Guyana) in 1803. Working for the Hudson's Bay Company, Douglas established Fort Victoria in 1843 and set about turning it into a center of political power. Sir James Douglas was knighted before he died aged 74.

1 Royal British Columbia Museum

This museum is known for its First Nations artifacts and art, as well a fascinating collection of highlights from BC's history and its natural wonders (see pp30–31). Changing exhibitions are highly thought-provoking.

2 Fairmont Empress Hotel

This luxury château-style hotel (see p119) was built by the Canadian Pacific Railway in 1908. The afternoon tea, served here daily, is a fine treat and an elegant experience.

3 Inner Harbour

The Inner Harbour (above) is the historic center of Victoria. A mix of yachts, fishing boats, ferries, and float planes dock here, while pedestrians happily stroll along a wide, curved walkway.

4 British Columbia Parliament Buildings

Impressive gray granite buildings house the provincial legislature. Overlooking the Inner Harbour, the Neo-Classical structure (below) is a wonderful sight at night, illuminated by 3,560 sparkling light bulbs.

5 Craigdarroch Castle

This four-story, 39-room stone mansion was built in the late 1880s for coal baron Robert Dunsmuir. Highlights include period furnishings, stained-glass windows **(above)**, and a grand oak staircase.

6 Beacon Hill Park

Noted for its gnarled Garry oak trees and 350-year-old Chinese bell, this park, dating from the mid-1800s, is a lovely place to stroll around and have a picnic.

7 Maritime Museum of British Columbia

This museum showcases BC's rich seafaring past, with 35,000 artifacts as well as informative walking tours of the Inner Harbour. Visitors can also learn about pirates and infamous shipwrecks, or try their hands at sailor's knot.

8 Emily Carr House

Built in 1864, the house that artist Emily Carr *(see p20)* was born in typifies the sensibilities of the Victorian era. The building has been described as both English Gingerbread and San Francisco Victorian, inspiring the restoration of many of the area's old houses.

9 Art Gallery of Greater Victoria

Housed in an 1889 mansion, this gallery is known for its Asian collection, including a Shinto shrine in the Asian garden. Paintings and literary work by local artist Emily Carr **(right)** are also featured.

10 Chinatown

The Chinatown in Victoria once rivaled San Francisco's for size. Today, the bustling two-block area is home to artists' studios, restaurants, and a wide range of shops.

NEED TO KNOW

Royal British Columbia Museum: **MAP P4**; 675 Belleville St; 1 888 447 7977; open 10am–5pm daily; closed Jan 1 & Dec 25; adm; www.royalbc museum.bc.ca

Inner Harbour: **MAP N3**

British Columbia Parliament Buildings: **MAP P4**; 501 Belleville St; 250 387 3046; open for guided tours 9am–5pm daily; www.leg.bc.ca

Craigdarroch Castle: **MAP E6**; 1050 Joan Cres; 250 592 5323; open mid-Jun– Labour Day: 9am–7pm daily, Labour Day–mid-Jun: 10am–4:30pm daily; adm; www.thecastle.ca

Beacon Hill Park: **MAP Q6**; 250 361 0600; www. victoria.ca

Chinatown: **MAP P1**; Fisgard & Herald Sts at Government St

Maritime Museum of British Columbia: **MAP P3**; 634 Humboldt St; 250 385 4222; open 10am–5pm daily (Sep–May: to 4pm Tue–Sat); adm; www. mmbc.bc.ca

Emily Carr House: **MAP P6**; 207 Government St; 250 383 5843; open May– Sep: 11am–4pm Tue–Sat; adm; www.emilycarr.com

Art Gallery of Greater Victoria: **MAP E6**; 1040 Moss St; 250 384 4171; open 10am–5pm Tue–Sat (to 9pm Thu), noon–5pm Sun; adm; www.aggv.ca

■ BC Ferries connect Vancouver with Victoria. BC Transit operate a large network of buses across the city *(see pp110–11)*.

■ A trip with Harbour Ferry *(250 708 0201, www. victoriaharbourferry.com)* is a great way to sight-see.

Royal British Columbia Museum

① First Peoples Gallery

Historic photos, video, audio, and First Nations artifacts are combined for a spellbinding experience in this gallery. Look out for the collection of superb ceremonial masks.

② Modern History Gallery

In the atmospheric 20th-Century Hall, it's easy to step back into the Victoria of the early 1900s. Re-created buildings include the Grand Hotel, with its authentic wood-cobbled street, a salmon cannery, a dressmaker's studio, and a Chinese herbalist's shop, all displaying authentic period objects. There's also a full-scale replica of Captain George Vancouver's H.M.S. *Discovery*.

③ Netherlands Centennial Carillon Tower

This tower, with 62 bells, was gifted to the museum in 1967 from BC residents of Dutch descent. Free recitals are usually held at 3pm on Sundays.

First Nations totem pole

④ Thunderbird Park

A dozen poles preside over this park. The carved mythical figures tell stories of traditional Coast Salish cultures. Included are Gitxsan memorial poles, Haida mortuary poles, a Cumshewa pole, and Kwakwaka'wakw heraldic poles.

⑤ Ocean Station

A Victorian-era "submarine" exhibit allows visitors to access BC's coastal marine life. Peer through portholes at kelp beds, watch live sea creatures, including sea urchins and fish, in the central 95-gallon (360-liter) aquarium, then check out the colorful vistas on a giant underwater cliff through a moveable periscope.

⑥ St. Ann's Schoolhouse

Built in 1844 and donated to the museum by the Sisters of St. Ann, this building was once a school classroom. It was moved to its current location in 1974 and is now an interpretive center.

⑦ Mungo Martin House

Also called Wawadit'la, this replica of a big house was built in 1952 by Chief Mungo Martin, who was considered the finest carver of his day, with the assistance of his family. The house posts bear the family's crest. Wawadit'la is a functioning big house and is still used for First Nations events with the permission of Chief Martin's grandson.

⑧ IMAX Victoria Theatre

Subjects as diverse as whales and outer space are explored in a series of documentary and feature films on the theater's six-story screen.

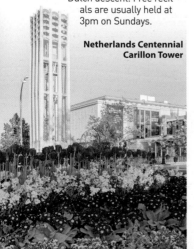

Netherlands Centennial Carillon Tower

9 Natural History Gallery

Realistic dioramas explore a range of environments, from ocean to boreal forest, including the giant old-growth forest that once covered coastal BC. One of the most striking of the range of animals depicted in re-created habitats is a grizzly bear, BC's largest land predator. Other highlights include full-size models of a woolly mammoth and a northern (or Steller) sea lion.

Exterior of the Helmcken House

10 Helmcken House

One of the oldest houses in BC still on its original site was built by Dr. John Sebastian Helmcken in 1852. The three-room log structure is made of Douglas fir trees. Period furnishings reflect the Victorian era.

RECONCILIATION AND REPATRIATION

In March 2017, The Royal British Columbia Museum organized a symposium in partnership with the First Peoples' Cultural Council. This gathering in Kelowna, BC, was to discuss the repatriation of indigenous ancestral remains, sacred objects and cultural heritage items in the museum's collection. Public attention has been focused on reconciliation with BC's First Nations since the Truth and Reconciliation Commission (TRC) of Canada revealed the harm done to the more than 150,000 Aboriginal, Metis and Inuit children removed from their communities and forced to attend residential schools. The TRC report reinforced the rights of indigenous peoples to restitution of their heritage, including many items now exhibited in museums across North America and Europe.

TOP 10 MUSEUM OBJECTS

1 Dinosaur footprints
Cast from imprints in Peace River Canyon.

2 Woolly Mammoth
This model is in the Natural History gallery.

3 Totem Hall
The central exhibit in the First Peoples Gallery.

4 Huu-ay-aht welcome figures
Pre-1900 carved figures are exhibited in the lobby.

5 Elza Mayhew sculpture
Mayhew's imposing totemic bronze "Caryatid."

6 Captain Cook dagger
The weapon that was used to kill the explorer.

7 Judge Begbie's wig
This was worn by BC's first supreme court judge.

8 Cougar
BC's largest wild cat is in the Coastal Forest diorama.

9 Haida box by Bill Reid
Bill Reid made this gold box in 1971.

10 Chinese tailoring shop
A reassembled shop in the Old Town.

Totem Hall features huge totem poles and carvings from the Heiltsuk, Kwakwaka'wakw, Nuxalk, Gitxsan, Haida and Nuu-chah-nulth communities.

TOP 10 ★ Around Long Beach

The wild west coast of Vancouver Island's Long Beach area offers pristine wilderness, old-growth rain forest, endless beaches, and mystical vistas. Bald eagles appear in large numbers in Clayoquot Sound, a UNESCO biosphere reserve, while the Pacific Ocean teems with Dall's porpoises, sea lions, and seals. Surfing, fishing, kayaking, and storm watching are superb.

1 Long Beach

Rolling waves thrash the sandy shores of this seemingly endless beach, 15.5 miles (25 km) in length. Temperate rain forests featuring giant Sitka spruce and cedars border the beach. The Pacific Ocean rollers offer year-round surfing.

GRAY WHALES

Each year, an estimated 20,000 gray whales migrate past the Vancouver Island coast around Long Beach. They are on an 11,000-mile (17,700-km) round trip, migrating south from the Arctic to their breeding grounds off southern California and Mexico from December to early February, and returning north from March through May.

2 Eagle Aerie Gallery

The cedar-planked Eagle Aerie Gallery in Tofino is a tranquil hand-hewn longhouse traditional to the local First Nations people. Internationally acclaimed Tsimshian printmaker Roy Henry Vickers is the gallerist.

Around Long Beach

Clayoquot Sound
Vancouver Island Range
Kakawis
Tofino Inlet
Tofino
Kennedy Lake
Kildonan
Ucluelet
Tzartus Island
Broken Group Islands
Sarita
Bamfield

3 Ucluelet

This small town is the gateway to multiple outdoor activities on both land and water **(below)**. Avid fishers flock here for steelhead, sturgeon, halibut, and Pacific and freshwater salmon. The climate is temperate, with 328 frost-free days a year.

Kwisitis Visitor Centre ④
Displays at this center **(right)** show the natural history of the area and introduce historic cultural objects of the local Nuu-chah-nulth people.

⑤ Wild Pacific Trail
This 10-mile (16-km) trail runs alongside the ocean through rain forest, from the tip of the Ucluelet peninsula to the Pacific Rim National Park.

⑨ Tofino
This pretty coastal town was named by Spanish explorer Juan Francisco de la Bodega y Quadra after one of his teachers, a hydrographer. Located at the entrance to Clayoquot Sound *(see p92)*, and with just 1,900 residents, Tofino provides easy access to beaches and is a magnet for outdoor adventurers, winter storm watchers, and foodies.

⑥ Meares Island
Accessed by boat or water taxi, visitors to Meares Island **(above)** can walk the Boardwalk Trail to the hanging garden tree, an ancient red cedar.

⑦ Pacific Rim National Park Reserve of Canada
This park, a famous spot for whale-watching, is made up of three distinct areas: Long Beach, the West Coast Trail, and the Broken Group Islands.

⑧ West Coast Trail
The West Coast Trail is a challenging 46-mile (75-km) hike along a historic path built to help shipwrecked mariners. Waterfalls, arches, and caves dot the rocky coast.

⑩ Hot Springs Cove
A popular outing 23 miles (37 km) northwest of Tofino is Hot Springs Cove **(above)**, reached by floatplane or boat. Stroll on a boardwalk through old-growth rain forest, before immersing yourself in one of the rocky geothermal pools.

NEED TO KNOW

Long Beach: **MAP A4**

Eagle Aerie Gallery: **MAP A4** ■ 350 Campbell St, Tofino; open 10am–5pm daily; www.royhenry vickers.com

Kwisitis Visitor Centre: **MAP B5**; 485 Wick Rd, Ucluelet; open 10am–5pm Fri–Sun (daily in summer)

Meares Island: **MAP A4**

Ucluelet: **MAP B5**; www. ucluelet.ca

Wild Pacific Trail: www. wildpacifictrail.com

Pacific Rim National Park Reserve of Canada: www. pc.gc.ca

West Coast Trail: www. westcoasttrail.com

Tofino: **MAP A4**

Hot Springs Cove: **MAP A4**

🔟⭐ Whistler

The 75-mile (120-km) drive to Whistler from Vancouver showcases stunning scenery, a combination of Howe Sound's sparkling blue waters and the majestic snow-covered Coast Mountain range. The magnificent side-by-side peaks of Whistler and Blackcomb mountains welcome more than two million visitors every year. A year-round resort, Whistler has hosted both the Olympic and the Paralympic Winter Games. While the resort is known for its hotels, restaurants, and shops, it still preserves five lakes and beautiful natural enclaves of forests.

1 Blackcomb Mountain

Nicknamed the "Mile High Mountain," Blackcomb towers over Whistler resort at an elevation of 7,494 ft (2,284 m). Skiers can choose from more than 100 marked runs. In summer, Horstman Glacier is unmissable.

2 Whistler Mountain

Skiers and snowboarders can enjoy 7.4 sq miles (19.3 sq km) of thrilling terrain with more than 100 marked trails **(right)**. Whistler Village Gondola offers superb views of Whistler Valley during the 20-minute ride to the top. Mountain biking and alpine hiking are great summer activities.

3 Fairmont Chateau Whistler

Whistler's grand dame **(above)** reigns over the valley from the Upper Village. The antique furnishings, gold-leaf ceiling, and Canadian art in the lobby of this chateau-style hotel make it well worth a visit. The opulent Mallard Lounge has a popular heated patio.

4 Whistler Village

This pedestrian-only Alpine-style enclave, ringed by shops, hotels, and restaurants, provides ski-in, ski-out access to Whistler Mountain. It's busy round the clock.

NEED TO KNOW

MAP F1

Whistler Visitor Centre:
4230 Gateway Dr; 604 935 3357; www.whistler.com

Fairmont Chateau Whistler:
4599 Chateau Blvd; 604 938 8000; www.fairmont.com

■ Take warm and waterproof clothing up the mountains, even during the summer.

■ Horstman Hut is the highest eatery in the area, sitting at 7,494 ft (2,284 m).

■ Watch out for black bears on the Valley Trail, especially in the early morning or evening. If you spot one, keep your distance and back away.

■ Ride PEAK 2 PEAK from Whistler to Blackcomb Mountains on one of the highest and longest gondolas in the world.

6 Valley Trail

The lovely 25-mile (40-km) Valley Trail **(left)** attracts walkers, cyclists, and in-line skaters. It leads past Lost Lake, Rainbow Park, and Alta, Nita, and Alpha lakes, through stands of trees that fringe residential areas. In winter, the Lost Lake loop is dedicated to cross-country skiing.

WHISTLER TRANSIT

A free shuttle travels every 20 to 30 minutes between village hotels and condos to the ski slopes. BC Transit buses take guests to and from the villages and around the town. Alternatively, call Whistler Taxi (604 932 3333) or use their app.

8 Upper Village

Nestled at the base of Blackcomb Mountain, the Upper Village offers easy access to the slopes. The ski-in, ski-out luxury hotels, restaurants, and shops are unsurpassed. In summer, Adventure Zone is great for kids.

9 Village North

Construction of Village North followed that of Upper Village, with the added attractions of vehicle access, a shopping mall, cafés, restaurants, and lifestyle shops.

5 Alta Lake

This area was once home to Rainbow Lodge, Whistler's first resort. Traces of it remain at Rainbow Park **(below)**. Explore the lake's perimeter on the paved Valley Trail, or, swim, wind surf, or canoe.

7 Creekside

A multimillion-dollar investment has transformed this activity center, providing chic hotels and a mini-mall. Skiers can access Whistler Mountain from this historic base at the Creekside Gondola.

10 Green Lake

A glacial gem with crystal-clear water thanks to mountain melt, Green Lake is spectacularly situated between some of the area's highest peaks, including massive Mount Currie.

The Top 10 of Everything

**Visitors walking the Cliffwalk at
Capilano Suspension Bridge Park**

🔟 Moments in History

① Around 6000 AD: First Nations Settle in Vancouver

For around 8,000 years, the Northwest Coast was a place of settlement for numerous Coast Salish peoples, including the Squamish, Tsleil-Waututh and Xwméthkwyiem, who once occupied what is now Vancouver. Vancouver Island is the traditional land of the Nuu-chah-nulth and Kwakwaka'wakw peoples, with the Lekwungen People (also known as the Esquimalt and Songhees Nations) in Victoria.

Illustration of Hudson's Bay Company

② 1790s: Arrival of the Europeans

Captain James Cook landed on the west coast of Vancouver Island in 1778, but both the island and the future city were to be named after British Captain George Vancouver, who explored Burrard Inlet in 1792. He visited only briefly, as at that time the Spanish had laid claim to the territory. European arrival and eventual settlement would prove devastating to the First Nations.

③ 1808: Simon Fraser Mistakes the Columbia River

In 1808 Simon Fraser set out to try to find a direct route for the fur trade to the Pacific. He followed what he thought was the Columbia River but, after a perilous expedition, he realized the river he had found emptied into the Strait of Georgia, so it couldn't possibly be the Columbia. The mouth of the Fraser River (as it became known) is the site of present-day Vancouver.

Captain James Cook sculpture, Victoria

④ 1821: Hudson's Bay Company

At the beginning of the 19th century, Canada experienced competition in the fur trade between the North West Company and the Hudson's Bay Company. In 1821 the companies merged, and in 1828 Hudson's Bay set up trading outpost Fort Yale on the Fraser River.

⑤ 1850s: Gold Fever

After gold was found in the Fraser River, Fort Yale underwent a population explosion. Rapid economic expansion in the region led to the area being declared a British Crown Colony.

⑥ 1868: Victoria becomes the Capital City

Fort Victoria was the hub of the fledgling province of British Columbia. During the Gold Rush all miners had to report there before receiving a license, and the city became a major seaport and trading centre. In 1868 the city was named British Columbia's capital.

7 1887: Canadian Pacific Terminus

A huge turning point in the fortunes of Vancouver was the decision to move the terminus of the Canadian Pacific Railway from Port Moody 14 miles (22 km) east, to what was then called Granville (and was quickly renamed Vancouver). The first train pulled in on May 23, 1887.

8 1908: University of British Columbia is Established

In 1899, Vancouver College was established, affiliated with Montreal's McGill University, and in 1908 the first steps toward an independent university were taken. Point Grey was the designated spot, but it took 17 years before its inauguration (see p103).

9 1986: Vancouver's Centennial

The centennial of the founding of Vancouver was 1986 and it was marked by Expo '86, (see p15) a World Fair that had a tremendous impact on the city. The legacy of Expo '86 endures today with SkyTrain, BC Place Stadium and Canada Place.

Canada Pavilion during Expo '86

10 2010: Winter Olympics and Paralympics

A joint bid between Vancouver and Whistler (see pp34–5), the Winter Games were based at the BC Place Stadium and cost close to $2 billion. As part of investment for the Games, the Sea-to-Sky highway was improved, the Canada Line transit to Richmond opened, and the Olympic Village was built.

TOP TEN FAMOUS VANCOUVERITES

Inspirational figure David Suzuki

1 Dr. David Suzuki
A contemporary scientist, broadcaster, and environmentalist, Suzuki inspires individuals to protect the natural world.

2 Pauline Johnson
Credited for naming Stanley Park's Lost Lagoon, Johnson (1861–1913) published First Nations legends and lore in English.

3 Joseph Seraphim Fortes
Joe came to Vancouver from Trinidad, via England, in 1885. As Vancouver's first lifeguard, he saved hundreds of lives.

4 Emily Carr
From Victoria rather than Vancouver, Carr's Modernist and landscape art features prominently in the Vancouver Art Gallery (see pp20–21).

5 Chief Joe Capilano
Sa7plek (Sahp-luk) or Kiyapalanexw (anglicized to Capilano) sought greater rights for indigenous peoples.

6 Michael J. Fox
A Hollywood A-list actor, Fox was diagnosed with Parkinson's disease in the 1990s and set up a non-profit foundation for Parkinson's research.

7 Douglas Coupland
Known for his 1991 novel Generation X, Coupland grew up in West Vancouver.

8 Michael Bublé
The singer and songwriter started out in a downtown club on Granville Street.

9 Seth Rogen
Aged just 16, Rogen and his family headed from Vancouver to LA to launch his career as an actor and producer.

10 Heather Ogden
Before becoming Principal Dancer at the National Ballet of Canada in 2005, Ogden trained at the Richmond Academy of Dance.

🔟 Museums and Art Galleries

Wood Interior by Emily Carr

1 Vancouver Art Gallery

The gallery's collection is rich in historic and contemporary works by BC and international artists, including the world's largest collection of Emily Carr pieces. The splendid *fin de siècle* exhibition hall hosts exhibits *(see pp20–21)*.

2 Chinese Cultural Centre Museum and Archives

MAP M4 ▪ 555 Columbia St ▪ 604 658 8880 ▪ Open Tue–Sun 10am–5pm ▪ Adm ▪ www.cccvan.com

The collection here tells the story of the Chinese community from the Cariboo Gold Rush to the settlement of Chinatown. The annex exhibits classical and modern Chinese art.

3 Roedde House Museum

MAP J3 ▪ 1415 Barclay St ▪ 604 684 7040 ▪ Open Jun–Aug: 11am–4pm Tue–Sat, 1–4pm Sun; Sep–May: 1–4pm Tue–Fri & Sun ▪ Adm

This is the only only museum in the city set in a heritage house, with original 19th-century architecture and beautifully restored artifacts. The museum regularly hosts small, intimate concerts.

4 BC Sports Hall of Fame and Museum

BC's sports achievements, including those of local heroes Terry Fox and his Marathon of Hope *(see 76)* and Rick Hansen's Man in Motion World Tour, are celebrated in this gallery space *(see p77)*. The Participation Gallery entices visitors to try out pitching, sprinting, and rock climbing.

5 Inuit Gallery

MAP L3 ▪ 206 Cambie St ▪ 604 688 7323 ▪ Open 10am–6pm Mon–Sat, 11am–5pm Sun ▪ www.inuit.com

One of the region's most respected commercial galleries, the Inuit Gallery shows an outstanding, museum-quality selection of Inuit and Northwest Coast First Nations sculpture, graphics, and jewelry.

6 Museum of Vancouver

Permanent and short-term exhibits offer an intimate look at Vancouver's heritage. Hands-on exhibits, such as the 1950s soda shop,

Futuristic exterior of the Museum of Vancouver

[Map showing downtown Vancouver with numbered locations: Alexandra Park, West End, English Bay, Vanier Park, Aquatic Centre, Granville Island Market, Fish Dock, Granville Island, False Creek, Yaletown, David Lam Park, Coopers' Park, Plaza of Nations, Science World, Pacific Central Station, Gastown, Chinatown, and surrounding streets. Scale: 0 meters/yards to 800.]

and a visit to the hippie era in Vancouver – complete with 1960s clothes to try on – make recent history a delight *(see p85)*.

7 Museum of Anthropology at UBC

Situated on cliffs overlooking Burrard Inlet, this museum has over 500,000 ethnographic and archaeological objects from around the world, with a focus on coastal First Nations *(see pp18–19)*.

Exhibit in the Museum of Anthropology at UBC

8 Bill Reid Gallery

One of Canada's greatest artists, Bill Reid (1920–98) helped to introduce the Northwest Coast's indigenous art traditions to a wider audience through his work. This gallery houses more than 60 pieces of his jewelry, and works by contemporary Inuit and First Nations artists *(see p77)*.

9 Vancouver Maritime Museum

Exhibits of artifacts, models, vessels, and photos pay tribute to Canada's marine heritage *(see p84)*. At the heart of the collection is the restored 104-ft (32-m) schooner *St. Roch*, the second ship to navigate the North West Passage, but the first to travel it from west to east.

10 Vancouver Police Centennial Museum

Enter the old city morgue, now the police museum's forensic laboratory, and it's not difficult to imagine the coroner leaning over the slab, about to start an examination. The 20,000 artifacts housed here offer an intriguing glimpse into the dark world of crime and punishment in Vancouver's past *(see p69)*. Exhibits include confiscated weapons, counterfeit bills, and displays showing scientific evidence. You may find yourself amid a gaggle of wide-eyed children, as school tours play an important part in the programming.

Vancouver Police Centennial Museum

🔟 First Nations Art

Bronze sculpture *The Jade Canoe* by Haida sculptor Bill Reid

1 The Jade Canoe
MAP A2 ■ Vancouver International Airport

Haida artist Bill Reid's awe-inspiring bronze creation is the second casting of *The Black Canoe*. Thirteen characters from Haida mythology paddle an imposing 20-ft (6-m) canoe.

2 Carved Doors

The entrance to the Museum of Anthropology at UBC is itself a work of art *(see p19)*. Made of red cedar by four Gitxsan master carvers, the double doors convey a narrative from the Skeena River region. When closed, the images form the shape of a Northwest Coast bentwood box, objects used by First Nations people for storage and burials.

3 Hetux
MAP A2 ■ Vancouver International Airport

Travelers at Vancouver airport are greeted by *Hetux*, a huge birch-and-aluminum sculpture. Connie Watts here combined the form of the mythical thunderbird with features of wolves, wrens salmon, and hummingbirds to reflect the untamed spirit of her grandmother.

4 Chief of the Undersea World

Orcas were still kept at the Vancouver Aquarium *(see p13)* when Haida artist Bill Reid's sculpture was installed outside it in 1984. The 16-ft- (5-m-) tall bronze killer whale leaping into the air remains as a tribute to this native West Coast creature.

5 Thunderbird House Post

A majestic thunderbird stands above a grizzly bear, which holds a human being. The house post is a replica of one of a pair carved in the early 1900s by artist Charlie James. After 40 years in Stanley Park, the deteriorated poles were restored and moved indoors. Carver Tony Hunt re-created the post now in the park's Brockton Point Visitor Centre *(see p13)*.

6 'Ksan Mural
MAP K3 ■ 1025 W Georgia St

Five artists carved this red cedar frieze showing Northwest Coast raven myths. The nine panels tell stories of how the Raven created the elements of the world through his mischievous activities.

Thunderbird House Post

7 One of the World's Tallest Totem Poles
MAP Q6

Raised in Beacon Hill Park *(see p29)* in 1956, the pole, by Kwakwaka'-wakw chief Mungo Martin with David Martin and Henry Hunt, took six months to carve from a 128-ft- (39-m-) tall cedar.

8 Kwakwaka'wakw Totem Pole

This pole, at Victoria's Royal British Columbia Museum *(see pp30–31)*, provides a chance to see a modern interpretation of traditional carving by Kwakwaka'wakw artists Jonathan Henderson and Sean Wonnock. The pole features a mythical thunderbird on top of the tail of an orca.

9 Coast Salish Welcome Figures
MAP A2 ▪ **Vancouver International Airport**

Two 17-ft- (5-m-) tall red cedar figures welcome airport arrivals in traditional Musqueam style. Northwest Coast artist Susan Point carved both from the same log.

Inukshuk sculpture by Alvin Kanak

10 Inukshuk
MAP G3 ▪ **English Bay Beach**

Made by Alvin Kanak for Expo '86, this granite sculpture is an Inuit welcome figure, a traditional traveler's marker, although much larger than those found in the Arctic.

TOP 10 PUBLIC ARTWORKS

A-maze-ing Laughter, **Morton Park**

1 A-maze-ing Laughter
MAP G3 & H4 ▪ Denman and Davie Sts
Crowds tend to gather around these playful figures in Morton Park.

2 Photo Session
MAP B2 ▪ Queen Elizabeth Park
Join Seward Johnson's family of bronze figures posing for a snapshot.

3 The Crab
MAP G4 ▪ 1100 Chestnut St
Admire George Norris's stylized stainless-steel sculpture of a crab.

4 Gate to the Pacific Northwest
MAP G4 ▪ Vanier Park
Alan Chung Hung's sculpture invokes 18th-century navigation instruments.

5 Douglas Coupland's Digital Orca
MAP K2 ▪ Vancouver Convention and Exhibition Centre
This piece captures the spirit of Vancouver's harborfront.

6 Salute to the Lions of Vancouver
MAP L2 ▪ 999 Canada Pl
Gathie Falk's steel lions align with Lions Gate Bridge and The Lions mountain.

7 Angel of Victory
MAP L3 ▪ 601 W Cordova St
Coeur de Lion MacCarthy's bronze angel lifts a World War I soldier heavenward.

8 Street Light
MAP K5 ▪ Marinaside Cres
Panels showing images of historic events cast shadows onto a walkway.

9 Pendulum
MAP K3 ▪ 885 W Georgia St
This stunning seven-story kinetic sculpture is by Alan Storey.

10 Inukshuk
MAP G3 ▪ English Bay
This stone statue became BC's emblem during the 2010 Winter Olympics.

ᴛᴏᴘ**10** Parks and Gardens

1 Pacific Spirit Regional Park

This huge park on Vancouver's west side (see p104), supports pine forests as well as birch, alder, cottonwood trees. Extensive trails cross the peninsula from Point Grey to the University of British Columbia (UBC). The park features beaches, bluffs overlooking the expansive Spanish Banks, and the Camosun Bog.

2 Bloedel Conservatory

MAP B2 ■ Queen Elizabeth Park, W 33rd Ave & Cambie St ■ 604 257 8584

Visitors to Canada's first geodesic conservatory are enveloped by steamy air as they step into this dome filled with desert and tropical plants. The calls of free-flying birds add to the exotic ambience.

3 Butchart Gardens

Starting in 1904, Mrs. Jenny Butchart created five spectacular gardens to beautify her huband's excavated limestone quarry on the outskirts of Victoria. Her first creation was the Japanese Garden. Next came the lush Sunken Garden. Some one million bedding plants blossom yearly, with 700 plant varieties (see p94).

Spring flowers in Beacon Hill Park

4 Beacon Hill Park

Since 1858, Beacon Hill has been the queen of Victoria's parks. Wooden bridges over a stream, a petting zoo, and an English-style rose garden add to the charm. Visitors can walk, ride horses, and picnic on the beach here (see p29).

5 Dr. Sun Yat-Sen Classical Chinese Garden

This gem of a park in Chinatown reflects the serenity of a Ming Dynasty garden (see p70).

Brightly colored plants and trees in the Butchart Gardens

6 David Lam Park

MAP J5

With a large expanse of green space, this Yaletown park has lots of private corners for sitting and relaxing, as well as playgrounds and sports courts.

7 Queen Elizabeth Park

This pretty park *(see p104)* in central Vancouver was once a stone quarry. The Quarry Garden is now its centerpiece. A small rose garden is planted with hardy varieties that blossom year-round.

8 Stanley Park

Cedar, hemlock, and fir trees are all dotted throughout this park *(see pp8–11)*. Old-fashioned roses and lush hybrid rhododendrons share space with cherry, magnolia, and dogwood trees, plus more. Park staff plant 350,000 annual flowers for year-round beauty.

Geese in a pond in Vanier Park

9 Vanier Park

English Bay is the backdrop for this expansive park near Granville Island. Largely treeless, the 37-acre area was named after Georges P. Vanier, governor general of Canada from 1959 to 1967 *(see p85)*.

10 VanDusen Botanical Garden

The array of flowers, shrubs, and trees here are unrivaled in Vancouver. Over 7,500 varieties from six continents enjoy the city's four distinct seasons. There are rolling lawns and peaceful lakes *(see p104)*.

TOP 10 BC TREES

Moss-covered Douglas Fir trees

1 Douglas Fir
The province's economy was built on the lumber from this imposing tree that grows to a height of 300 ft (90 m).

2 Yellow Cedar
Growing in colder elevations, the soft wood from this tree is the ideal choice for First Nations carvings.

3 Western Red Cedar
Dark, scale-like needles mark the down-swept branches of this sometimes huge evergreen tree.

4 Hemlock
The most common tree on the West Coast, hemlock is easily recognizable by its droopy top branches.

5 Sitka Spruce
The Carmanah Giant, a Sitka spruce on Vancouver Island is, at 312 ft (95 m), the tallest recorded tree in Canada.

6 Arbutus
Peeling red-brown bark identifies the arbutus, also known as the madrona, the only broad-leafed evergreen tree native to Canada.

7 Pine
Straight lodgepole and Ponderosa pines grow at higher elevations.

8 Dogwood
The white or pink flowers of this tree bloom in spring, and famously appear on BC's official coat of arms.

9 Japanese Flowering Cherry
More than 40,000 of these blossoming trees line Vancouver's streets; many were given as a gift from Japan.

10 Maple
Canada's national tree grows in bigleaf, Douglas, and vine varieties. Bigleaf wood is often used for First Nations canoe paddles.

🔟 Beaches and Bays

1 English Bay

This beautiful bay is a popular West End attraction. On New Year's Day it hosts the Polar Bear Swim, when thousands of swimmers brave the cold waters. A more popular year-round activity is to walk the Seawall that runs beside the bay into Stanley Park *(see p12)*, fueled with caffeine or ice cream from nearby Davie and Denman street cafés.

2 Rathtrevor Beach Provincial Park

MAP C4

Parksville's beautiful Rathtrevor Beach is easily accessible and great for watersports. Swim in the warmest saltwater north of California, build sandcastles, dig clams, canoe, or camp along the 4 miles (7 km) of sand.

3 Jericho Beach

MAP A1 ■ Windsure Adventure Watersports: 604 224 0615

This family-friendly beach has an outdoor shower and changing rooms for freshening up after a day of splashing around in the water. Picnics on the beach are a favorite pastime. For the more adventurous, windsurfing lessons are available at Windsure Adventure Watersports.

4 Long Beach

On the west coast of Vancouver Island, between Tofino and Ucluelet, Long Beach *(see pp32–3)* is beautiful even on a cloudy day – there are some visitors that come in the winter months specifically to watch the powerful Pacific surf pound the headland. On summer days, the serenity of the vast empty beach is perfect for a long stroll at low tide.

Sunset Beach in Vancouver

seaside town that shares its name. It is a great place to watch sunsets.

8 Lighthouse Park

Park in the convenient lot or hop off the bus and enjoy a short walk though West Vancouver's 500-year-old forest to the shore. There are some wonderful coastal views from the 1912 Point Atkinson Lighthouse. Eagle Point, on the east side of the bluff, also has stunning vistas across Burrard Inlet to Vancouver *(see p104)*.

5 Sunset Beach

This designated quiet beach is along the Seawall, at the mouth of False Creek. It is not far from downtown and – as the name suggests – it's a gorgeous place to watch the sun set. Vancouverites come here to watch the world go by from cafés along the waterfront or to catch the sun on the small but lovely stretch of sand *(see p83)*.

6 Spanish Banks Beach
MAP A2

This is the longest expanse of sandy beach in Vancouver, and is split into three sections: Spanish Bank East, Spanish Bank West, and Spanish Bank Extension. At low tide, the water can be up to 0.5 miles (1 km) off-shore. The beaches are popular with walkers, cyclists, picnickers, and families splashing in the tidal waters.

7 Qualicum Beach
MAP C4

Beachcombers and kayakers love this curved sandy beach and the

The sandy shore of Long Beach

Point Atkinson Lighthouse

9 Kitsilano Beach and Park

MAP B2 ■ Kitsilano Pool: 2305 Cornwall Ave; 604 731 0011

"Kits" Park, linked by a tree-lined walk to the beach, is favored by swimsuit-clad volleyball players and sunbathers. The busy Olympic-size Kitsilano Pool overlooks the beach.

10 Wreck Beach
MAP A4

Getting to this clothing-optional beach is easy via a steep trail leading down from SW Marine Drive on the UBC campus. The hard part is the climb back up. Beware: oglers on the beach are conspicuous. There are spectacular views to be had across the Strait of Georgia toward Vancouver Island *(see p55)*.

🔟 Spas

Reception area in the Spa at Four Seasons Resort Whistler

1 Silk Road Spa
MAP P1 ▪ 1624 Government St, Victoria ▪ 250 382 0006
This organic spa takes its cue from China, where tea and relaxation balance each other to harmonious effect. Green tea, an antioxidant, is used in some of the treatments.

2 Grotto Spa
MAP C4 ▪ Tigh-Na-Mara Seaside Resort and Spa, 1155 Resort Dr, Parksville ▪ 250 248 1838
Overlooking an expanse of beach, BC's largest spa resort offers a wide range of treatments, including couple's massages. Their signature body treatments can include Canadian glacial clay, sea salt, and seaweed.

Pool at the Grotto Spa

3 Spa at Four Seasons Resort Whistler
MAP F1 ▪ 4591 Blackcomb Way, Whistler ▪ 604 935 3400
Eucalyptus steam rooms at this sparkling, high-ceilinged spa offer total relaxation. Treatments feature Canadian maple syrup and seaweed.

4 Vida
Located in the Fairmont Chateau Whistler (see p34), this spa has specialists in Ayurvedic massage analyze clients for the best way to treat their *dosha*, or body composition, using ancient holistic techniques. Staff then balance the *dosha* with dry brushing, a steam in the cedar cabinet, and essential oil massages.

5 Spa at the Wedgewood
The specialty at this spa at the Wedgewood Hotel (see p116) is the Chai Soy anti-stress back treatment, which also includes a relaxing scalp and foot massage. The cinnamon enzyme facial, with its skin tightening effect, is also a favorite.

6 Spa Utopia
MAP K2 ▪ 1001-999 Canada Pl ▪ 604 689 7700
Awaken your senses at Spa Utopia with their signature facial that uses

hot stones and Japanese facial techniques or experience the detoxifying Canadian Moor Mud body wrap.

(7) Absolute Spa at the Century

Escape into relaxation at this plush, award-winning spa at the Century Plaza (see p117). Choose from a soothing Hawaiian coconut lomi lomi massage, skin purification with Italian mandarin oil, or a rejuvenating oxygen facial.

(8) Willow Stream Spa

The signature treatment here, Island Senses, includes a pine hydrotherapy bath and a restoring massage with aromatic lavender oil. The spa's setting is as romantic as the hotel it is located in – the sumptuous Fairmont Empress Hotel (see p119).

Treatment room at Willow Stream Spa

(9) skoah

MAP J5 ■ 1007 Hamilton St ■ 604 901 3335

Skin care is the main focus at this luxurious spa. Its personalized Facialiscious treatment is the most requested. Skin-calming plant extracts are mixed by a staff chemist.

(10) Scandinave Spa Whistler

MAP F1 ■ 8010 Mons Rd, Whistler ■ 604 935 2424

This wonderful retreat is a haven of peace and quiet. Hydrotherapy is at the core of what they do and stages include hot eucalyptus steam baths and a wood-burning sauna, then cold plunge baths to flush out toxins.

TOP 10 HEALTH AND BODY TREATMENTS

Relaxing hot stone massage

1 Hot Stone Massage
Locally sourced basalt rocks are heated and applied to the body to eliminate stress and restore energy.

2 Seaweed Wraps
West Coast seaweed mud remineralizes the body. Followed by an application of hot towels, a wrap makes skin feel wonderfully soft all over.

3 Plant Extracts Facial
Plants such as refreshing cucumber are blended with extracts, including gingko biloba and St. John's Wort, in creams that make the skin glow.

4 Couple's Massage
Sessions for couples focus on full-body relaxation massages by two therapists working side by side.

5 Body Lufa Exfoliation
Organic lufa is ground into a fine dust and essential oils are carefully massaged into the skin in order to hydrate and improve circulation.

6 Ayurvedic Steam Cabinet
A steam in a cedar cabinet is an aromatic way to detoxify.

7 Aromatherapy
Aromatic oils are blended for their mental and physical effects, often with a hint of cedar, pine, or lavender.

8 Spray Tan
Hydrating, nourishing products are used to apply even, sun-free color.

9 Therapeutic Body Massage
This therapeutic massage combines deep compressions with yoga-like stretches for energy and calm.

10 Lomi Lomi
This is a traditional full-body Hawaiian massage with free-flowing, wave-like strokes, which relaxes the body.

🔟 Children's Attractions

Visitors waiting in line for entry to Vancouver Aquarium in Stanley Park

1 Vancouver Aquarium
Canada's largest aquarium (see p13) introduces kids to everything from eels and octopuses to tropical fish in re-created natural habitats. Naturalists are on hand to answer questions. Special events for kids include sleepovers with the sea lions.

2 H. R. MacMillan Space Centre
Kids here can touch a moon rock, watch star shows, morph into an alien, or climb aboard a spacecraft and let the motion simulator replicate the feeling of space travel (see p84).

H. R. MacMillan Space Centre

3 OMNIMAX® Theatre
Watching films on the massive five-story screen situated in the Science World building (see pp26–7) will make children feel like they are right in the middle of the action.

4 Science World
Kids can play with the displays at this hands-on discovery center and they won't even know they're learning something. Science World (see pp26–7) also has healthy fast-food dining.

5 Stanley Park
The miniature railway at Stanley Park makes a fun 15-minute excursion. From March through October, the park (see pp12–13) also offers horse-drawn tours, which are relaxing and cover many of the popular spots. Kids can also play a round of golf at the pitch-and-putt course. Second Beach has a play area, a swimming pool, and a beach.

6 Grouse Mountain
There's more than skiing and snowboarding at Grouse (see p101). In summer try hiking, zip-lining, paragliding, guided eco-walks, or riding the Skyride to the top. At the Refuge for Endangered Wildlife, see peregrine falcons, gray wolves, and grizzlies. Loggers throw axes and roll logs at the lumberjack show.

Granville Island Water Park

MAP H5/6 ▪ 1318 Cartwright St ▪ 604 257 8195 ▪ Open summer only (check the website) ▪ www.falsecreekcc.ca

Kids will love splashing in the cool spray, shooting water cannons, and zooming down water slides at this large water park. There are changing rooms and bathrooms in the False Creek Community Centre next door.

8 Capilano Suspension Bridge Park

Walk the swaying bridge, then climb Treetops Adventure's boardwalks and platforms perched high in the forest at this park *(see pp16–17)*.

9 Playland and the Pacific National Exhibition

MAP B2 ▪ 2901 E Hastings St ▪ Playland: open summer (hours vary, check website); adm ▪ Pacific National Exhibition: 604 253 2311; open mid-Aug–early Sep; www.pne.ca

With rides for all ages, Playland is always a hit with children. Highlights include its famed wooden roller coaster and climbing wall. During the Pacific National Exhibition, held on the same site as Playland, many additional rides are available. The exhibition also features monster truck races and demolition derbies.

Milking activity at Maplewood Farm

Maplewood Farm

MAP C1 ▪ 405 Seymour River Pl ▪ 604 929 5610 ▪ Adm ▪ www.maple woodfarm.bc.ca

Kids enjoy pony rides, sheep shearing, and mingling with the animals at this farm. There is a picnic area, a greenhouse, and an aviary, too.

TOP 10 PLACES TO EAT WITH KIDS

1 Old Spaghetti Factory
53 Water St ▪ 604 684 1288
Pastas and other Italian dishes are served in an old warehouse themed around Gastown in the 19th century.

2 Topanga Café
2904 W 4th Ave ▪ 604 733 3713
A laid-back Vancouver favorite serving California-style Mexican food from a menu that children can color in.

3 Sophie's Cosmic Café
2095 W 4th Ave ▪ 604 732 6810
This place has 1950s decor with booths and big portions of comfort food.

4 Rocky Mountain Flatbread Co.
1876 W lst Ave ▪ 604 730 0321
Organic pizzas and a play area for kids; parents can relax with good wine.

5 Café Deux Soleils
2096 Commercial Dr ▪ 604 254 1195
This vegetarian place is where hip young families come to meet and eat. There's a great toddlers' play area.

6 Go Fish
1505 W 1st Ave ▪ 604 730 5040
This tiny seafood shack offers some of the best fish and chips in the city.

7 Aphrodite's
3605 W 4th Ave ▪ 604 733 8308
This eatery offers organic brunch and has high chairs and crayons for kids.

8 Burgoo
4434 W 10th Ave ▪ 604 221 7839
This comfort food bistro, with a sunny little patio, offers a special kids' menu.

9 Boathouse
1795 Beach Ave ▪ 604 669 2225
A beachfront restaurant serving a West Coast menu along with a kids' menu.

10 White Spot
405 Dunsmuir St ▪ 604 899 4581
Classic burgers and fries are available here, as well as healthier choices.

Sign for White Spot Restaurant

TOP 10 Entertainment Venues

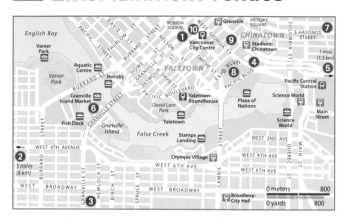

1 The Orpheum
MAP K4 ■ 601 Smithe St ■ 604 665 3035 ■ www.vancouver civictheatres.com

Restored to Baroque grandeur, the Orpheum is a lush, former Vaudeville palace built in 1927. Vancouver Symphony Orchestra and choral concerts, rock shows, and other musical events are performed here in the acoustically upgraded space.

Seating in Chan Shun Concert Hall

2 Chan Centre for the Performing Arts
MAP A2 ■ 6265 Crescent Rd, University of British Columbia ■ 604 822 9197 ■ www.chancentre.com

In this striking, three-venue, cylindrical center, music is performed in the glorious 1,200-seat Chan Shun Concert Hall, whose adjustable acoustic canopy allows all types of music to sound their very best. A small experimental theater and a cinema round out the entertainment venues.

3 Stanley Theatre
MAP B2 ■ 2750 Granville St ■ 604 687 1644 ■ www.artsclub.com

This 1930s movie house was restored to its former elegance in the 1990s. It is now home to the Arts Club Theatre Company, who perform dramas, comedies, and musicals here.

4 Rogers Arena
MAP L4 ■ 800 Griffiths Way Pacific Blvd N at Abbott St ■ 604 899 7400 ■ www.rogersarena.com

Home to the Vancouver Canucks National Hockey League team, this huge arena is also one of the busiest entertainment venues in North America: since 1995, the stadium has hosted some 170 concerts and events each year.

5 Vancouver East Cultural Centre
MAP B2 ■ 1895 Venables St ■ 604 251 1363 ■ www.thecultch.com

Canadian and international theater and dance, as well as local and world music, are all presented in this renovated 1909 Methodist church, which now has a studio stage. The "Cultch" is one of the first LEED (Leadership in Energy and Environmental Design) certified arts centers in Canada.

6 Granville Island Stage/ Revue Stage

MAP H5 ■ Revue Stage: 1601 Johnston St, 604 687 1644 ■ www.artsclub.com

The Arts Club Theatre Company's 440-seat Granville Island Stage and its more intimate 198-seat Revue Stage, prove theatre doesn't have to be formal. New and classic comedies, dramas, and musicals are featured at both venues.

7 Firehall Arts Centre

MAP M3 ■ 280 E Cordova St ■ 604 689 0926 ■ www.firehallarts centre.ca

Built around 1906, this heritage fire station is now an innovative Gastown theater featuring modern, often culturally diverse plays, many by home-grown talents. The 175-seat studio theater includes an outdoor stage and a cozy licensed lounge bar.

8 BC Place Stadium

MAP L4–L5 ■ 777 Pacific Blvd ■ 604 669 2300 ■ www.bcplace.com

This stadium features the world's largest cable-supported retractable roof. Football is the main attraction, with BC Lions games held here, as well as big concerts and trade shows.

Lights at BC Place Stadium

Concert at Queen Elizabeth Theatre

9 Queen Elizabeth Theatre and Vancouver Playhouse

MAP L4 ■ 630 Hamilton St ■ 604 665 3050 ■ www.vancouvercivictheatres. com

Home to the Vancouver Opera and Ballet BC, and hosting many guest artists, the Queen Elizabeth Theatre is located in a 1960s-built, Modernist venue. Adjacent to it, the Vancouver Playhouse Theatre Company hosts dance and music shows and events.

10 Commodore Ballroom

Since 1929, eclectic national and international acts have performed here, from Sammy Davis Jr. to The Police, U2, and Katy Perry, as well as Canadian and world music performers (see p79).

TOP10 LGBT Vancouver

Patio for alfresco drinking and dining at Score on Davie

1 Fountainhead Pub
MAP J4 ▪ 1025 Davie St ▪ 604 687 2222

With its excellent selection of lagers on tap and appetizing menu, the Fountainhead Pub is a good first stop when hitting Davie Village. It's a great place to watch sports play-offs on TV.

2 Celebrities
Brilliant lighting and visuals, state-of-the-art sound, and the city's hottest DJs and performers get the crowd – gay, straight, bi, and curious – moving. Apply to the online guest list and you can skip the line *(see p79)*.

3 Score on Davie
MAP H3 ▪ 1262 Davie St ▪ 604 632 1646

This sports bar and grill is known for its friendly welcome, casual vibe and great patio space. Brunch is provided until 2pm every day – try a Caesars (similar to a Bloody Mary cocktail) and tuck into an enormous portion of fried delights. There's also a fantastic range of craft ales and bottled lager. Popular sports events and themed parties are hosted here regularly.

4 The Elbow Room Café
MAP H4 ▪ 560 Davie St ▪ 604 685 3628

This long-standing brunch spot is known for its eclectic breakfast and brunch menu, spiced up with the sarcastic, humorous and unconventional service of the staff.

5 Delany's Coffee House
MAP H2 ▪ 1105 Denman St ▪ 604 662 3344

Perhaps the city's most popular see-and-be-seen coffee house, this place has a good-sized patio.

Dancer at Celebrities nightclub

6 Little Sister's Book & Art Emporium

MAP H3 ▪ 1238 Davie St
▪ 604 669 1753

If there is an anchor to Vancouver's gay community, Little Sister's is it. More than a bookstore, it's a long-standing institution that has taken Canada Customs to the Supreme Court of Canada in its fight for freedom from censorship. There's a good selection of literature, event tickets, gift items, clothing, DVDs, and various play things.

Sunbathers on Wreck Beach

7 Sunset Beach and Wreck Beach

A few blocks southwest of Davie Village, Sunset Beach (see p83) is popular with runners and cyclists, or those strolling with a coffee in hand. In summer, volleyball players fill up the sandy beach. While located at the bottom of UBC cliffs, secluded Wreck Beach (see p47) is thronged with people who enjoy sunbathing *au naturel*. There are several steep but maintained trails, and during the warmer months vendors sell refreshments and beach fare.

8 Davie Village

MAP H3

With its fuchsia bus shelters and trash bins, Davie Village is Vancouver's gay 'hood. Located in the West End between Burrard Street and Jervis Street, it's a lively 24-hour strip with cafés, an excellent selection of shops (including sex shops), gay clubs, and restaurants for all budgets and tastes, not to mention its plethora of trendy bars.

9 1181

MAP J3 ▪ 1181 Davie St
▪ 604 787 7130

This sleek and modern lounge is lined with comfortable couches and illuminated with many little lights. Enjoy the extensive cocktail list served by friendly bartenders.

10 Numbers Cabaret

MAP J4 ▪ 1042 Davie St ▪ 604 685 4077

This fun, friendly, and unpretentious gay club is usually packed with people from all walks of life. There's something for everyone, including pool tables, darts, DJs pumping out club classics and the latest tunes across five dance floors, and Karaoke Funbox in the loft every night. Ongoing events include cabaret nights and drag shows. Daily drinks specials feature extravagant cocktails and jugs of beer.

🔟 Bars and Clubs

Dark wood and exposed brick interior of the bar at Diamond

1 The Diamond

This second-floor bar and restaurant in hip Gastown has a sophisticated feel with high ceilings and soft lighting. Known for craft cocktails and sushi, it's a great spot for a date night. You can also see DJs dusting off their vinyl records here Sunday through Thursday *(see p72)*.

2 Celebrities

A legendary Vancouver nightspot in the heart of Davie Village. Although officially catego-rized as a gay bar, Celebrities is popular across the spectrum and

DJ booth at Celebrities

is simply a great place to dance. Music styles vary across the week and include hip-hop, R&B, funk, rock, retro, and house *(see p79)*.

3 Venue

In the heart of the Granville Street club district, Venue has a 12,000 sq-ft (1,115 sq-m), two-level room with a glam-rock inspired interior. Weeknights feature live shows, while on the weekend the city's top alternative DJs spin pop, rock, and retro originals, along with bass-heavy electro mixes *(see p79)*.

4 The Irish Heather

This gastropub serves up good food, including many pub favorites, in a casual and friendly setting *(see p64)*. Shebeen – a whiskey house offering a great selection of about 100 single malts, bourbon, rye, scotch, and whiskey – is located in this building.

5 The Bimini

2010 W 4th Ave ■ 604 733 7116

Enjoy modern pub food and local craft beers at this well-established pub in the Kitsilano neighborhood. The dance floor gets lively with locals in the evening. You can also watch live sports on big-screen TVs and play arcade games and pool.

6 The Keefer Bar

With a patio and a funky decor, this swanky and sleek Chinatown cocktail bar is the perfect place to unwind. It offers medicinal-sounding drinks and Asian inspired cocktails alongside late-night dim sum snacks and fusion small plates. The music is a mix of soul, hip-hop, and funk, and it also features live music (see p72).

7 Commodore Ballroom

Opened in 1926, this club has seen many musical eras. Catch one of the many great acts and test out the room's bouncy sprung floor. Updated, and always on the cutting edge of music, the Commodore Ballroom lives on as the city's great-grandfather of clubs (see p79).

8 Guilt & Co.

This cool little place hosts nightly live performances in an easily missed basement venue beneath the Local in Gastown. Make sure you get there early as they operate a one-in-one-out policy to avoid overcrowding. Indulge in some great cocktails and choose from their extensive whiskey menu (see p72).

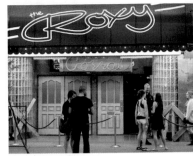

Legendary club The Roxy

9 The Roxy

A Vancouver institution, The Roxy (see p79) hosts top Canadian and local bands and is a favorite nightspot of Vancouver Canuck's hockey team. Line-ups at this popular club are common after 9pm, so be warned and get in line early.

10 Granville Island Brewing

The taproom at the center of the brewery that started Vancouver's craze with small-batch handcrafted beer is on bustling Granville Island (see pp24–5). Since 1984 they've been all about natural ingredients and West Coast inspiration – they'll even advise on the best beers to drink along with the brewery's delicious food, which is made exclusively using local produce.

Granville Island Brewing

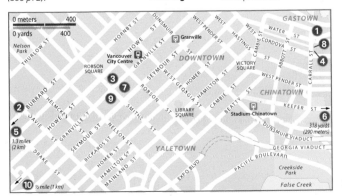

🔟 Restaurants

Interior at Blue Water Café

flavors and techniques combined with West Coast elements create an innovative menu, with sustainable seafood recognized by the Ocean Wise conservation program. It has a bar, lounge area and full-service sushi bar (see p73).

1 Blue Water Café

The freshest and finest wild seafood is served in a 100-year-old brick-and-beam warehouse. The decor is contemporary, the atmosphere friendly, and the kitchen serves mouth watering delicacies such as sablefish in soy and ginger broth (see p89). The Raw Bar is the domain of a master sushi chef..

2 Miku

This Japanese eatery is known for its gourmet *Aburi* (flame-seared sushi), complemented by an elegant setting. Traditional Japanese

Beautifully presented food at Chambar

3 Tacofino

With humble beginnings as a food truck in Tofino on the west coast of Vancouver Island, this is a taco hotspot in several locations, including Gastown's Blood Alley (see p73). You can tuck into delicious and filling burritos, or sip margaritas and craft beers on the sunny patio. The menu also offers a range of tacos, nachos, and churros. They also have happy hours.

4 Chambar

Success hasn't spoiled this Belgian restaurant in the Crosstown neighborhood (see p73). It is one of the hottest eateries in town and perenially packed to the rafters. Traditional dishes such as *moules frites* excel, but for a real treat try the *Congolaise* version, where mussels are cooked in a tomato and coconut cream sauce with smoked chili and lime.

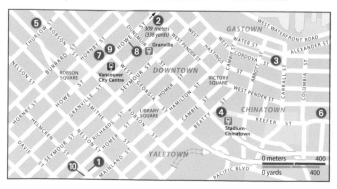

Softly lit dining area at CinCin Ristorante & Bar

5 CinCin Ristorante & Bar

The Italian-inspired menu of this inviting space includes dishes from the wood-fired oven. If you're not in a rush, order the melt-in-your-mouth free-range chicken cooked under a brick in the wood-fired oven for 25 minutes. The drinks menu features 1,000 wines *(see p81)*.

6 Bao Bei

Locals rave about the lamb sirloin sliders, heavenly dumplings, and innovative small plates at this Chinese brasserie *(see p73)*. Bao Bei does not take reservations, so arrive early. With advance notice, groups of eight to twelve can enjoy a tasting menu at the large family table.

7 Diva at the Met

Chef Hamid Salimian is a master of molecular gastronomy, serving up innovative cuisine from Diva's open kitchen *(see p81)*. His unique offerings include puffed *foie gras* in caramelized fig.

8 YEW Seafood + Bar

If you're after something a bit fancy from the Pacific Northwest, then elegant YEW is the place *(see p81)*. Dishes change seasonally, and the choice of sustainable and wonderfully presented farm- and ocean-to-table delicacies might include steamed Dungeness crab, lobster bisque or Ahi tuna.

9 Hawksworth

Situated in an elegant room at the Rosewood Hotel Georgia, this gem has garnered multiple awards for its dazzling food and star chef David Hawksworth. The *foie gras*, roasted lamb, and rib-eye steak dishes are all outstanding in terms of presentation and flavor *(see p81)*.

Plush dining tables at the Hawksworth

10 Cioppino's Mediterranean Grill

Inventive *cucina*-style dishes are made with fresh vegetables and low-fat sauces for a tasty meal that is easy on the waistline. Or choose the succulent natural beef short ribs braised in red wine. A great wine list rounds out the experience *(see p89)*.

For a key to restaurant price ranges see p73

TOP 10 Shopping Destinations

Interior of the huge Metropolis mall at Metrotown

2 Robson Street

Chic Robson Street's shopping epicenter (see p76) is at the corner of Burrard and Robson, where Lululemon and Roots Canada make their homes. Shop for clothing at Canadian-owned Aritzia pick up some bath products in Lush, or browse internationally known clothing, shoe, accessory, and home furnishing stores. Take a breather at any of the many restaurants en route.

1 Metrotown

MAP C2 ■ **4700 Kingsway, Burnaby** ■ **604 438 4715**

Metropolis at Metrotown is BC's largest mall. The atmosphere is lively with many shoppers visiting daily. The Hudson's Bay department store and the grocery giant Superstore anchor the mall, with chains and independents represented by nearly 400 stores. There are movie screens and arcade games for non-shoppers.

3 South Granville

MAP H6

In South Granville, shopping extends along Granville Street from 2nd to 16th avenues. At least a dozen art galleries are found here. The elegant strip is home to brand-name and high-end European clothing purveyors such as Bacci's, Boboli (see p87), and MaxMara. Excellent tea and coffee shops, home decor showrooms, and toy stores are found along this strip, too.

4 Commercial Drive

MAP B2

The Drive, as it's known locally, is the epitome of a hip area. Once Vancouver's Little Italy, it is now a multiethnic mix of clothing shops, book and magazine stores, vintage boutiques, and second-hand outlets. To make the most of your visit, start at East Broadway and Commercial Drive and walk north to Venables Street, admiring the distant Coast Mountains along the way.

⑤ Sinclair Centre
MAP L3 ■ 757 W Hastings
■ 604 488 1685

Four heritage buildings are grouped to create an upscale shopping mall. The three levels include two floors of exclusive shops offering luxury clothing and accessories from the likes of Versace, Zuhair Murad, Prada, and Alexander McQueen. The lower level has a food fair.

⑥ Granville Island
There's more to shopping on the Island than just fresh foods at the Public Market: look for silver jewelry and hats among the stalls *(see p86)*. The Net Loft – once used for fishing net repairs – sells crafts and handmade paper. The Kids Market offers mini-shops and activities for the little ones.

Stall at Granville Island Public Market

⑦ Broadway
MAP A1–B1

Shopping hotspots on Broadway are located between Main and Alma streets. Mountain Equipment Co-op, at the eastern end, requires a small membership fee, but the sportswear is superb. Going west, the street is dotted with clothing stores and health food stores, particularly at Granville, Arbutus, and Macdonald streets (the latter is home to the city's Greektown).

⑧ Pacific Centre
MAP K3 ■ 701 W Georgia St
■ 604 688 7235

More than 100 stores stretch beneath Granville Street in the heart of downtown Vancouver, including department stores, boutiques and specialty stores selling clothing, jewelry, sportswear, gadgets, and more.

Shopping street in Chinatown

⑨ Chinatown
Vancouver's oldest and largest ethnic shopping area has struggled at times to survive with competition from Richmond's Asian supermalls. Yet Chinatown hangs on, its crowded streets filled with bargain hunters. Shops selling herbs and potions, exotic delicacies, fresh seafood and vegetables, leather goods, and Asian souvenirs fill the streets *(see p70)*.

⑩ Gastown
The century-old buildings of Gastown have morphed into one-of-a-kind boutiques, First Nations art galleries, and specialty shops selling everything from buttons to cowboy boots. Gastown *(see p69)* has long been known for its souvenirs, and many retailers selling classic and kitsch Canadiana line Water Street.

Cowboy boots in a shop in Gastown

🔟 Vancouver and Vancouver Island for Free

Art Deco detail in the Marine Building

1 Marine Building
MAP K3 ▪ 355 Burrard St

Close to Canada Place (which can of course also be explored for free), this 1930s building is adored by those in the know. It was once the tallest building in the British Empire, with mesmerizing Art Deco details in the grand entrance, lobby and elevators. Entrance to the lobby is free on weekdays between 8:30am and 5pm.

2 The Seawall
The city's famed greenway (see p12) offers epic views, picnic spots, and beaches along its 28-km (17.5-mile) route. The stretch around Stanley Park is one-way only.

3 Gaze at the Stars
The observatory at the H. R. MacMillan Space Centre (see p84) is free for stargazing from 7pm until 11pm every Saturday. Donations are welcome.

British Columbia Parliament Buildings

4 Christ Church Cathedral
With the motto "Open Doors, Open Hearts, Open Minds" Christ Church Cathedral (see p75) can be visited for free all week, but Choral Eucharist (at 10:30am on Sundays) is when the custom-built Kenneth Jones organ and award-winning choir can be heard.

5 Free Walking Tours
Vancouver City Council: www.vancouver.ca/publicart ▪ Tour Guys: www.tourguys.ca

There are several downloadable brochures for fascinating self-guided public art walking tours on the Vancouver City Council website. You can also book free city walking tours on the Tour Guys website (although the guides do appreciate a tip at the end of the tour).

6 British Columbia Parliament Buildings
Victoria's imposing Neo-Classical 19th-century Parliament building (see pp28–29) is home to the legislative Assembly of British Columbia. Free public tours run on weekdays when Parliament isn't sitting (check the website for times) and you don't need to book. However, for speciality tours that focus on the architecture or formal gardens you must reserve a place in advance.

7 Lynn Canyon Park

This expansive park (see p102) is a lush green space with walking trails and swimming holes, plus a 50-m (165-ft) suspension bridge. The entire site, including the ecology centre, can be visited free of charge.

8 International Buddhist Temple

MAP B3 ▪ 9160 Steveston Hwy, Richmond (25 mins from downtown) ▪ www.buddhisttemple.ca

Chinese culture and heritage, and Buddhist philosophy, is celebrated at Richmond's International Buddhist Temple (see p103), which is open to all. Don't miss the formal gardens, which can also be explored for free.

International Buddhist Temple

9 Free Admission

Some of Vancouver's best museums and galleries throw open their doors for free on certain days (a donation of whatever you can afford is appreciated). Head to Vancouver Art Gallery (see pp20–21) 5–9pm on Tuesday nights, the Museum of Vancouver (see p85) 5–9pm on the last Thursday of the month, and the Bill Reid Gallery (see p77) 2–5pm on the first Friday of the month.

10 Free Festivals and Events

Vancouver and the surrounding area host plenty of free festivals and events in every season, such as the largest fireworks festival in the world, an open-air concert at the end of the jazz festival, and Pride (see pp64–5). Canada Day on July 1 is celebrated with a huge fireworks display that lights up that waterfront (see p15).

TOP 10 BUDGET TIPS

Beacon Hill Park in Victoria

1 Spend time taking it easy for free in many of Vancouver and Victoria's excellent parks and gardens (see pp44–5).

2 Some of the best afternoon and early evening happy hours are at Royal Dinette (see p81), Medina Café (see p81), and L'Abattoir (see p73).

3 Save money on public transit costs in the city by buying all-zone day passes, or by getting books of ten tickets for the price of eight.

4 Take the Canada Line from the airport to downtown for less than $10.

5 Visit and explore year-round farmers' markets (www.eatlocal.org) that are free and offer inexpensive food options.

6 T&T supermarket is the place to stock up on inexpensive Asian staples and they often have free samples (www.tnt-supermarket.com).

7 For cheap dining, find out where the city's best food trucks are.

8 A Vancouver ($25) or Victoria City Passport ($20) offers money-off coupons for major tourist attractions (www.citypassports.com).

9 Purchase cheap same-day tickets for events from community box office Tickets Tonight at the Tourism Vancouver Visitor Centre (see pp14–15).

10 Sign up with Hostelling International before you travel to get access to all the best value hostels (www.hihostels.com). Unaffiliated hotels do sometimes offer discounts for members, too.

🔟 Festivals and Events

Members of the public enjoying Vancouver International Jazz Festival

1 Vancouver International Wine Festival

604 872 6623 ▪ Late Feb–early Mar
▪ www.vanwinefest.ca

From humble beginnings in 1979, the VanWineFest now hosts premier industry names and is considered to be one of the biggest, best, and oldest wine events in the world. It features wine tastings, gourmet dinners, seminars, and culinary competitions.

2 Concord Pacific Dragon Boat Festival

False Creek ▪ 604 688 2382
▪ Mid-Jun ▪ www.vancouverdragon
boatfestival.ca

Over 5,500 paddlers from around the world gather for a weekend of fun. There's more to do than just watch the races. Food, exhibits, and entertainment abound. Admission to Science World is included in the ticket price.

Concord Pacific Dragon Boat Festival

3 Vancouver International Jazz Festival

604 872 5200 ▪ Late Jun–early Jul
▪ www.coastaljazz.ca

Jazz in every imaginable style is presented in some 400 concerts at various venues around town. The event wraps up with an outdoor multistage free weekend.

4 Bard on the Beach Shakespeare Festival

MAP G4 ▪ Vanier Park ▪ 604 739 0559
▪ Jun–late Sep ▪ www.bardonthe
beach.org

Western Canada's largest professional Shakespeare festival, Bard on the Beach presents works by the Bard and related events.

5 Vancouver Folk Music Festival

MAP A1 ▪ Jericho Beach Park ▪ 604
602 9798 ▪ Mid-Jul ▪ www.thefestival.
bc.ca

Canadian and international acts play on open-air stages. The waterside park hosts nearly 30,000 folk music fanatics for three evenings and two full days of non-stop music.

6 Honda Celebration of Light

Jul & Aug ▪ www.hondacelebration
oflight.com

The night skies fill with fireworks, accompanied by broadcasted music, as three countries compete to win top bragging rights. Huge crowds flock to English Bay, Vanier Park, Kitsilano, Jericho, and West Vancouver beaches, so go early to snag a good spot.

7 Vancouver Pride Festival
604 687 0955 ■ Late Jul–early Aug ■ www.vancouverpride.ca

For two weeks, LGBTQ2+ people (and anyone who likes a good party) gather in the city's West End to celebrate diversity. The festival is a bevy of picnics, dances, cruises, breakfasts, and a grand finale parade and beach party, with thousands in attendance.

Float at Vancouver Pride Parade

8 Vancouver International Film Festival
604 683 3456 ■ Early Oct

More than 150,000 people gather at the city's annual film festival, which includes a strong showing of films from Canada and the Pacific Rim.

9 JFL NorthWest Comedy Festival
Early Mar ■ www.jflnorthwest.com

Expect generous doses of stand-up, sketch comedy, improvisation, and street performances by top Canadian and international comedians.

10 Vancouver Writers Fest
MAP H5 ■ Granville Island ■ 604 681 6330 ■ Mid-Oct ■ www.writersfest.bc.ca

International and Canadian writers attract throngs of readers to forums, readings, and literary cabarets in English and French. Writers stay on the festival site, so there's a decent chance you'll chat to a celebrity author.

TOP 10 PERFORMING GROUPS

1 Firehall Arts Centre
This theater group puts on entertaining shows, often with a multicultural twist *(see p53)*.

2 Ballet British Columbia
Ticketmaster: 1-855-985-5000.
World-class ballet shows are performed under bold leadership.

3 Vancouver Recital Society
604 602 0363
The VRS has a reputation for innovation and excellence in its programming.

4 Vancouver Opera
604 683 0222
This famous company puts on grand-scale productions of traditional and contemporary pieces.

5 The Dance Centre
604 606 6400
Traditional and contemporary dance performances from around the globe.

6 Early Music Vancouver
604 732 1610
The group plays concerts of works by medieval to late-Romantic composers.

7 Arts Club Theatre Company
Contemporary drama is performed by this group at Granville Island Stage and the Stanley Theatre *(see pp52–3)*.

8 Vancouver Theatresports League
604 738 7013
A great improv-based comedy group at Granville Island's Improv Centre.

9 Kokoro Dance Company
604 662 7441
Distorted movement and great intensity characterize Kokoro's *butoh*, a postwar Japanese dance form.

10 Vancouver Symphony Orchestra
604 876 3434
This wonderful orchestra performs world-class orchestral music.

Vancouver Symphony Orchestra

Vancouver and Vancouver Island Area by Area

The Lost Lagoon at Stanley Park and Vancouver Skyline

TOP 10 Waterfront, Gastown, and Chinatown

The Waterfront is Vancouver's Heart. It is one of the largest and busiest ports on the continent. With the opening of the cruise-ship terminal at Canada Place in the mid-1980s, it also became one of the world's major cruise-ship ports. A block away is Gastown, its origin as a tough mill town masked by graceful heritage buildings built in the boom years of the early 1900s. From here it is just a short walk to Chinatown, now home to over 35,000 people of Chinese descent, though its prosperity did not come easily – it was once seen as a threat by seasonal workers, and a closed-door immigration policy was imposed in 1885. Today, Chinatown attracts throngs of shoppers looking for authentic Chinese food and souvenirs.

Gassy Jack statue, Gastown

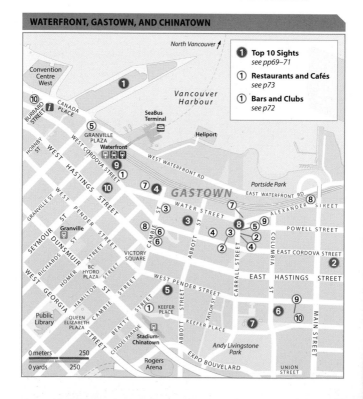

WATERFRONT, GASTOWN, AND CHINATOWN

① **Top 10 Sights**
see pp69–71

① **Restaurants and Cafés**
see p73

① **Bars and Clubs**
see p72

Canada Place, with its five sails, lit up at dusk

1 Canada Place

When Canada Place opened in 1986, it was greeted with controversy. Critics said its five "sails" were a poor imitation of Australia's Sydney Opera House. Today, the landmark complex is now a key player on the waterfront that has grown up around it *(see pp14–15)*.

2 Vancouver Police Centennial Museum

MAP M4 ■ 240 E Cordova St ■ 604 665 3346 ■ Open 9am–5pm Tue–Sat ■ Adm

Housed in the former Coroner Court, built in 1932, this museum *(see p41)* traces the fascinating history of the Vancouver Police Department. Real examples of criminal evidence are exhibited, including counterfeit money, antique firearms, and street weaponry. Always popular is the knife room. Unsolved murders are depicted in displays complete with dummies and period costumes.

3 Gastown

MAP L3–M3

The cobblestone streets of Gastown have been through many reincarnations. The current one is perhaps the most satisfying. Since the 1970s, the area has worked hard to better itself. The plethora of tawdry souvenir shops have largely been replaced with boutiques selling the work of local designers, a concentration of excellent First Nations and Inuit art galleries, restaurants, and clubs.

4 Steam Clock

MAP L3 ■ Water St at Cambie St

Said to be the first steam-operated clock in the world, this landmark is one of the most photographed in the city. However, the clock is not an antique. Local horologist Raymond Saunders built this 16-ft- (5-m-) tall clock in 1977 at the corner of Water and Cambie streets, basing it on an 1875 model. Be patient, and wait to hear the Westminster Quarters chime melody that plays every 15 minutes, along with mighty puffs of steam.

Steam Clock in Gastown

AN IRON ROAD, COAST TO COAST

The grand saga of Canadian railways is a tale of power and pain. In 1886, Prime Minister John A. Macdonald fulfilled his promise to build a cross-Canada railway to unite the new Dominion of Canada. The first transcontinental passenger train arrived in Vancouver on May 23, 1887, where Waterfront Station now stands. The whole city came out to celebrate the completion of the "Iron Road." Even the ships in the harbor were decked out in flags. Sadly, progress came at the loss of many lives, including more than 600 Chinese laborers.

Dr. Sun Yat-Sen Chinese Garden

5 Sun Tower
MAP L4 ▪ 100 W Pender St

A Vancouver landmark, the 17-story Sun Tower was the tallest building in the British Commonwealth, at 270 ft (82 m), when it was built in 1911. The handsome Beaux Arts building's nine nude statues once scandalized the city, but people turned out in droves in 1918 to watch Harry Gardiner, the "Human Fly," scale its walls.

6 Chinatown
MAP L4–M4

Stretching from Gore Avenue west to Carrall Street between Pender and Keefer streets, Chinatown dates to the 1880s and the building of the Canadian Pacific Railway, when as many as 20,000 Chinese came to Canada. Today it is North America's third-largest Chinatown. The Millennium Gate straddles Pender near Taylor Street and is the best place to start a walking tour of this lively area.

7 Dr. Sun Yat-Sen Classical Chinese Garden
MAP M4 ▪ 578 Carrall St ▪ 604 662 3207 ▪ Open daily (Nov–Apr : closed Mon) ▪ Adm

This Ming Dynasty-style garden, the first built outside China, opened in 1986. It re-creates the private areas typically found in a Ming scholar's home. With its meandering paths, corridors and courtyards, and asymmetrically placed rocks, the garden invites contemplation on the beauty and rhythm of nature. Plants include local and traditional Chinese varieties, such as flowering gingko trees and twisted pines.

8 Maple Tree Square
MAP M3 ▪ Water St at Carrall St

The city of Vancouver has its roots in this small square. Standing atop his barrel of beer, the statue of John "Gassy Jack" Deighton commemorates Gastown's founder. The talkative

Maple Tree Square, Gastown

publican built the city's first saloon with the help of thirsty sawmill workers. A maple tree here was once a popular meeting place until it was destroyed in the Great Fire of 1886. Gaoler's Mews was the site of the city's first prison, as well as the home of the city's first policeman, Constable Jonathan Miller.

⑨ Waterfront Station
MAP L3 ▪ **601 W Cordova St**

The station has been a transportation hub since 1887, when the original timber structure welcomed the first cross-Canada passenger train. The present white-columned building, which has Vancouver Harbour as its backdrop, was built in 1914.

The towering Vancouver Lookout

⑩ Vancouver Lookout
MAP L3 ▪ **555 W Hastings St**
▪ **604 689 0421** ▪ **Open May–Oct: 8:30am–10:30pm; Nov–Apr: 9am–9pm** ▪ **Adm**

The highlight of the Harbour Centre complex is its 581-ft (177-m) tower, home to an observation deck. The ride up in the glass-fronted elevator takes a thrilling 40 seconds. From the enclosed viewing deck, the 360-degree view is splendid. On a clear day, you can see Vancouver Island to the west and Washington State's Mount Baker to the south.

A DAY IN WATERFRONT, GASTOWN, AND CHINATOWN

Canada Place
Waterfront Station
Steam Clock
The Pourhouse
Maple Tree Square
Revolver
Chinese Cultural Centre Museum and Archives
The Irish Heather
Millennium Gate
The Keefer Bar
Dr. Sun Yat-Sen Classical Chinese Garden
Bao Bei

▶ MORNING

Begin your day at **Canada Place** (see pp14–15) for a great view of the harbor. After strolling the promenade for about half an hour, walk east to **Waterfront Station**, peeking at the scenic murals inside. From the junction of Cordova and Water streets, continue two blocks along Water Street to Cambie Street to admire Gastown's **Steam Clock** (see p69), then stop at hip Gastown café **Revolver** (see p73) for coffee. Enjoy an architectural walking tour before heading off to The **Irish Heather** (see p72) or **The Pourhouse** (see p72) for lunch.

AFTERNOON

Walk to **Maple Tree Square**, at Water and Carrall streets, to see the bronze statue of "Gassy Jack," the famous proprietor of the city's first saloon. From East Cordova, head south on Carrall Street to the peaceful **Dr. Sun Yat-Sen Classical Chinese Garden**. Spend 30 minutes here, then another half hour at the adjoining **Chinese Cultural Centre Museum and Archives** (see p40). Head east on Pender Street, admiring **Millennium Gate** as you walk through it into Chinatown. Spend the afternoon exploring the shops, looking out for the wooden heritage buildings you pass. End the day feasting on delicious Chinese food at **Bao Bei** (see p73). End the evening with a cocktail from **The Keefer Bar** (see p72) next door. Avoid wandering further east toward the lower part of Main Street – Vancouver's seedy side.

See map on p68 ←

Bars and Clubs

Bar and dining area at Steamworks Brewing

1 Steamworks Brewing
MAP L3 ▪ 375 Water St ▪ 604 689 2739

Complement your pizza, pasta, burger, or poutine with one of the several delicious beers brewed here, such as pale ale, lager, or porter.

2 The Irish Heather
MAP M4 ▪ 210 Carrall St ▪ 604 688 9779

There are about 200 single malts and Irish whiskeys to pick from in this pub. Tasty pub favorites include bangers 'n' mash *(see p56)*.

3 The Pourhouse
MAP L3 ▪ 162 Water St ▪ 604 568 7022

This evocative 1910 venue is steeped in history. There's low lighting, a chilled atmosphere, and a selection of clever cocktails and pub food.

4 The Blarney Stone
MAP M4 ▪ 216 Carrall St ▪ 604 687 4322

Friday and Saturday nights guarantee a rip-roaring, feet-stomping crowd at this legendary Irish pub and nightclub.

5 The Diamond
MAP M3 ▪ 6 Powell St ▪ www.di6mond.com

The bygone-era Diamond offers a cool and sophisticated setting in which to enjoy an extensive list of upscale craft cocktails *(see p56)*.

6 The Cambie
MAP L3 ▪ 300 Cambie St ▪ 604 684 6466

Pouring drinks since 1887, The Cambie serves mainly thirsty 20-somethings these days. Cheap microbrews are the big draw.

7 Guilt & Co.
MAP M3 ▪ 1 Alexander St ▪ 604 288 1704

This dimly lit underground live music venue has a refined but unfussy food and drinks menu. Wednesday is jazz night and weekends feature a rotation of high-energy bands *(see p57)*.

8 Alibi Room
MAP M3 ▪ 157 Alexander St ▪ 604 623 3383

DJs play funk, soul, and hip-hop in this two-level space with craft beers on tap. Catch art shows and movie screenings in the lower lounge.

9 The Keefer Bar
MAP M4 ▪ 135 Keefer St ▪ 604 688 1961

Situated in the heart of Chinatown, this cocktail bar serves creative drinks and snacks *(see p57)*.

10 Lobby Lounge
MAP L3 ▪ 1038 Canada Pl ▪ 604 695 5300

See and be seen at the Fairmont Pacific Rim's stylish lounge bar, which features live music by local artists.

Restaurants and Cafés

1 Chambar
MAP L4 ▪ 568 Beatty St ▪ 604 879 7119 ▪ $$$

Moules frites are the specialty at this hugely popular Belgian restaurant, where the cocktail menu is a great way to start the evening (see p58).

2 Tacofino
MAP L3 ▪ 15 W Cordova St ▪ 604 899 7907 ▪ $

This Mexican-inspired eatery, which has grown up fast since its days as a food truck in Tofino, still serves the original fish taco that is considered the best in town (see p58).

3 L'Abattoir
MAP M4 ▪ 217 Carrall St ▪ 604 568 1701 ▪ $$$

L'Abattoir offers fine dining in an informal setting of refurbished brick and beam. The menu has French-influenced West Coast fare at its best.

Chic interior of L'Abattoir

4 Salt Tasting Room
MAP L3 ▪ 45 Blood Alley ▪ 604 633 1912 ▪ $$

Tucked away in historic Blood Alley, this restaurant specializes in artisan cheeses, small-batch cured meats, and a really dynamic array of wines, sherries, and ports.

PRICE CATEGORIES

For a three-course meal for one with half a bottle of wine (or equivalent meal), taxes, and extra charges.

$ under $35 $$ $35–85 $$$ over $85

---

5 Miku
MAP L3 ▪ Suite 70–200 Granville St ▪ 604 568 3900 ▪ $$

With an atmospheric waterfront setting, this restaurant offers fresh, sustainable fish, specializing in flame-seared *Aburi* sushi (see p58).

6 Meat & Bread
MAP L3 ▪ 370 Cambie St ▪ 604 566 9003 ▪ $

The excellent sandwiches served here draw crowds, so expect long, yet fast-moving queues during lunch.

7 Al Porto Ristorante
MAP L3 ▪ 321 Water St ▪ 604 683 8376 ▪ $$

Pastas, fish, meat, and pizza are the highlights at this lively Italian *trattoria*. More than 300 wines are on offer.

8 Revolver
MAP L3 ▪ 325 Cambie St ▪ 604 558 4444 ▪ $

Baristas who are deadly serious about the roasting and brewing process serve coffee in this trendy exposed-brick café. This is not the place to ask for a caramel Frappuccino.

9 The Birds & The Beets
MAP M3 ▪ 55 Powell St ▪ 604 893 7832 ▪ $

This cozy café uses organic and local ingredients to serve simple dishes, including lovely avocado on toast.

10 Bao Bei
MAP M4 ▪ 163 Keefer St ▪ 604 688 0876 ▪ $$

In Bao Bei's sophisticated dining room, a savvy take on Chinese home cooking is the order of the day. Start with one of the expertly crafted cocktails available at the bar (see p59).

See map on p68 ←

🔟 Downtown

Originally a logging settlement surrounded by swamps, mills, and a few taverns, Vancouver's Downtown core has transformed and emerged as a sophisticated urban landscape with gleaming office towers, luxury boutiques, bustling shopping malls, and outstanding restaurants. The wide streets are lined with grand landmark buildings, vintage theaters, and fine art galleries. Downtown is always alive with a frenetic pace of activity, while the well-dressed locals rush about to relax and finish their day with a cocktail at one of the happening neighborhood lounges. Extending from Stanley Park and the West End to the west, to the historic districts of Gastown and Chinatown to the east, this area can be easily explored on foot.

Haida artist Bill Reid's totem pole at Brockton Point, Stanley Park

DOWNTOWN

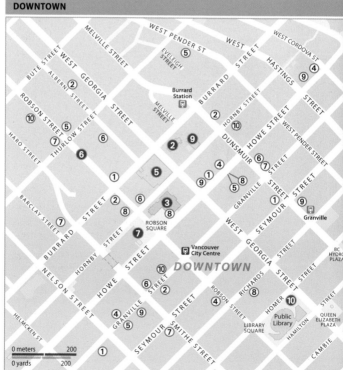

① Stanley Park

This 1.6 sq miles (4 sq km) of tamed wilderness is the green lungs of the city. The park *(see pp12–13)* is crisscrossed with trails and cultural landmarks, including Coast Salish gateways, totems at Brockton Point, and the life-size sculpture *Girl in a Wetsuit*. The Seawall circumnavigates it all and provides a perfect space for walking and cycling with stunning ocean views.

Interior of Christ Church Cathedral

② Christ Church Cathedral

MAP K3 ▪ 690 Burrard St ▪ 604 682 3848

A gem in the heart of the city and once a beacon for mariners entering

Vancouver's harbor, Christ Church Cathedral, consecrated in 1895, was designed in the Gothic Revival style. The interior has impressive old-growth Douglas fir ceiling beams and 32 stunning stained-glass windows; three in the office vestibule are by the British artist William Morris. Outside stands a 100-ft (30-m) tower of steel, clad with stained glass by Canadian artist Sarah Hall.

Greater Vancouver

0 km 2
0 miles 2

Stanley Park ①

Lost Lagoon

Burrard Inlet

③

English Bay

③ *Area of main map*

WEST END

③ GASTOWN

③

CHINATOWN

Vanier Park

YALETOWN

⑧

GRANVILLE

Creek ④

False Creek

⑩

VICTORY SQUARE

STREET

BEATTY ST

CITADEL PARADE

① **Top 10 Sights**
see pp75–7

① **Restaurants**
see p81

① **Bars and Clubs**
see pp79

① **Shopping**
see pp78

① **Cheap Eats**
see p80

***Big Raven*, Vancouver Art Gallery**

③ Vancouver Art Gallery

When the Court House was erected in 1912, designed by Francis Rattenbury, one of BC's flashiest architects, its solid form symbolized the British Empire at its very peak. Another controversial architect, Arthur Erickson, supervised the building's redesign in the mid-1980s when it became the Vancouver Art Gallery. Inside, the Emily Carr collection is Canada's largest, and includes the work *Big Raven*. Contemporary photoconceptual work also has a prominent place *(see pp20–21)*.

4 Science World

The striking geodesic dome housing Science World's interactive galleries and traveling exhibitions was built for Expo '86. Visitors can play with magnetic liquids, touch animal skin, and check out exhibits on motion and energy, as well as laser shows. The OMNIMAX® Theatre's giant screen fits into the dome's curves (see pp26–7).

Futuristic exterior of Science World

5 Fairmont Hotel Vancouver

MAP K3 ▪ 900 W Georgia St ▪ 604 684 3131 ▪ www.fairmont.com

Begun in 1928 by the Canadian Pacific Railway, construction on the city's most famous hotel halted with the 1929 stock market crash. Its steel skeleton sat until 1939, when it was hastily finished for the visit of King George VI. Features include a steep copper roof with impish gargoyles.

Stroll through the lobby and enjoy afternoon tea or a drink in the lounge, while admiring the lavish surrounds.

6 Robson Street

MAP H2–K4

West End residents, the city's urban chic, international celebrities, and tourists alike flock to Robson Street to join the bustle of shoppers (see p60). Part of the fun is people-watching over a specialty coffee, then browsing the brand-name and independent Canadian and international shops. Slip down a side street to get a taste of the historic West End, Canada's most densely populated area.

7 Robson Square and Law Courts

MAP J4 ▪ 800 block Robson St ▪ 604 660 8989

Spanning several blocks and four levels, Robson Square was designed by BC architect Arthur Erickson. On the south side of Robson Street, a cascading waterfall and trees cool the steps near *Spring*, a red steel sculpture by Alan Chung Hung. On the level above is a pond with seating. Jack Harman's sculpture, *Themis Goddess of Justice*, presides over the Great Hall, with its expanses of glass.

Cascading waterfall in Robson Square

TERRY FOX'S MARATHON OF HOPE

Born in Winnipeg in 1958, Terry Fox grew up in a Vancouver suburb. When just 18 years old, he was diagnosed with bone cancer and had his leg amputated. Three years later, in 1980, Terry dipped his artificial leg into the Atlantic, starting his Marathon of Hope across Canada to raise money for cancer research. After 143 days and 3,339 miles (5,373 km) Terry stopped. Cancer had spread to his lungs. He died in 1981, just after realizing his dream of raising $1 for every Canadian – over $24 million. A memorial to Terry Fox now stands at BC Place.

BC Sports Hall of Fame and Museum

8 BC Sports Hall of Fame and Museum

MAP L4 ■ 777 Pacific Blvd S, Gate A
■ 604 687 5520 ■ Adm

Twenty galleries showcase BC's sports history from the 1860s onward in a 20,000-sq-ft (1,858-sq-m) space located in BC Place Stadium (see p53). Interactive displays provide fascinating details of the lives of famous athletes, such as skier Nancy Green and sprinter Harry Jerome. The Participation Gallery is especially fun for kids.

9 Bill Reid Gallery

MAP K3 ■ 639 Hornby St
■ Open 10am–5pm daily ■ 604 682 3455 ■ www.billreidgallery.ca

Haida artist, master carver and gold- and silversmith Bill Reid blazed a trail for First Nations artists (see p41). The small public gallery named after him is dedicated to contemporary Indigenous Northwest Coast art, and temporary exhibits are thoughtful and far-reaching. A permanent gallery of his works, "Restoring Enchantment," exhibits a 28-ft (8.5-m) bronze frieze.

10 Library Square

MAP K4 ■ Corner of Robson & Homer sts

The Vancouver Central Library, partly designed by renowned architect Moshe Safdie, opened in 1995. At first criticized by some for its resemblance to a Roman amphitheater, it soon became universally popular. Library Square takes up a whole city block, and includes the library; a glass-roofed promenade; the Federal Tower, housing government offices; souvenir shops, a coffee bar, and takeout restaurants.

A DOWNTOWN WALK

▶ **MORNING**

Start at **BC Place Stadium** (see p53), exploring the **BC Sports Hall of Fame and Museum** for about an hour. Exiting the museum, head west toward **Robson Street**, passing by the four bronze statues of the **Terry Fox Memorial**, each bigger than the last, a tribute to the local hero who raised millions of dollars for cancer research. Continue west three blocks along Robson to Homer Street and **Library Square**. Drop in to have a look at the building's airy promenade before walking west on Robson to **Pacific Centre**. Browse the shops until lunchtime, then exit the mall and cross Howe Street to the **Vancouver Art Gallery** (see pp20–21). Enjoy a salad and sandwich in its casually elegant Gallery Café (see p80), snagging a patio table if the weather permits.

AFTERNOON

After lunch, head to the fourth floor of the Vancouver Art Gallery and take in the wonderful Emily Carr collection. Begin by watching the 15-minute video about this remarkable painter of forests and totem poles. Exiting the gallery, cross Robson and stroll through lovely **Robson Square**. Then indulge in some retail therapy in the various shops and boutiques on Robson Street. Satisfy a sweet tooth at one of the several chocolate shops. End the day with a fabulous dinner at **Gotham Steakhouse** (see p81). Treat yourself to the best steak in the city, while appreciating the Art Deco heritage surroundings.

See map on pp74–5 ←

Shopping

1 Roots Canada
MAP J3 ▪ 1001 Robson St ▪ 604 683 4305

Come here for Canadian-designed sportswear and leatherwear, including a wide range of classic accessories, from watches to belts and backpacks.

2 lululemon athletica
MAP J3 ▪ 970 Robson St ▪ 604 681 3118

This Vancouver-based company sells wildly popular yoga apparel, athletic gear, and casual wear.

3 Bute Street Liquor Store
MAP J3 ▪ 1155 Bute St ▪ 604 660 4569

This large BC liquor store carries an extensive variety of well-displayed wines, spirits, beers, and BC ice wine, made from frozen grapes.

4 Rendezvous Art Gallery
MAP K3 ▪ 323 Howe St ▪ 604 687 7466

The contemporary and traditional Canadian paintings and sculptures at this gallery reflect West Coast beauty. First Nations and Inuit artists are well represented.

5 Daniel Le Chocolat Belge
MAP J3 ▪ 1105 Robson St ▪ 604 688 9624

Belgian chocolate and all-natural or organic ingredients are used to create the delicious pralines and decadent champagne, coffee, and lemon truffles sold here.

6 Holt Renfrew
MAP K3 ▪ 737 Dunsmuir St ▪ 604 681 3121

This uniquely Canadian brand dates back to the early 1800s. The iconic Vancouver luxury fashion department store offers in-store boutiques, including Louis Vuitton and Chanel.

7 Aritzia
MAP K4 ▪ 1110 Robson St ▪ 604 684 3251

The haunt of trendy Vancouverites, Aritzia is a homegrown store selling cool clothing and accessories.

8 MAC Cosmetics
MAP J3 ▪ 908 Robson St ▪ 604 682 6588

A Canadian original, this is one of the world's leading cosmetic manufacturers known for its wide range.

9 Murchie's Tea & Coffee
MAP K3 ▪ 815 W Hastings St ▪ 604 669 0783

The Murchie family began selecting and selling fair-trade tea and coffee on the West Coast in 1894 and the tradition continues today.

10 John Fluevog Boots & Shoes Ltd
MAP K4 ▪ 837 Granville St ▪ 604 688 2828

Fluevog's funky, trendy, yet sturdy shoes and boots are always being snapped up by the fashion savvy.

John Fluevog Boots & Shoes Ltd

Bars and Clubs

The chic liquor-lined bar area at Prohibition

1 Prohibition
MAP J4 ■ 801 W Georgia St
(entrance off Howe St) ■ 604 673 7089
A green light is lit when this stylish prohibition-era-style bar at the Rosewood Hotel Georgia is open.

2 Commodore Ballroom
MAP K4 ■ 868 Granville St
■ 604 739 4550
A Vancouver institution since 1929, this club hosts popular ticketed rock, pop, blues, and jazz acts (see p57).

3 Celebrities
MAP H4 ■ 1022 Davie St ■ 604 681 6180
Punters line up around the block for entry to this hugely popular club (big name DJs sell out quick). The sound system is meant for dancing, not chat.

4 Caprice Nightclub
MAP K4 ■ 967 Granville St
■ 604 685 3288
Enjoy top 40 and retro nights at this club with a huge dance floor.

5 Republic
MAP K4 ■ 958 Granville St
■ 604 669 3214
Hip-hop and house is the mainstay at this gritty downtown nightclub, but club-within-a-club The Annex often hosts something a bit different.

6 Venue
MAP K4 ■ 881 Granville St
■ 604 646 0064
Live bands and a great balcony draw crowds to this trendy spot (see p56).

7 UVA Wine & Cocktail Bar
MAP K4 ■ 900 Seymour St ■ 604 632 9560
A European-inspired café by day and a chic lounge by night, that offers tapas and seasonal cocktails. Live jazz on Saturdays.

8 Yew Seafood + Bar
MAP K3 ■ 791 W Georgia St ■ 604 692 4939
The bartenders mix drinks like performance artists at this chic bar in the Four Seasons Hotel. Food is served on a communal dining table.

Interior of the Yew Seafood + Bar

9 The Roxy
MAP K4 ■ 932 Granville St
■ 604 331 7999
Where the locals go to dance to local and Canadian bands. Arrive early during the weekends (see p57).

10 Dubh Linn Gate
MAP M4 ■ 1601 Main St ■ 604 449 1464
A stone's throw from Science World, this Irish pub has quiz nights, live music, local craft ales and, of course, Guinness on tap. There's also a decent gastropub menu.

See map on pp74–5 ←

Cheap Eats

① The Fish Shack
MAP J4 ▪ 1026 Granville St
▪ 604 678 1049 ▪ $$

With seafood as fresh as the crowd that dines here, this casual eatery is fun and inexpensive. Their daily "buck a shuck" oysters is a good deal.

Fresh produce at the Urban Fare grocery store

② Urban Fare
MAP J3 ▪ 1133 Alberni St ▪ 604 648 2053 ▪ $

The restaurant at this gourmet grocery store serves salads, soups, and a sumptuous buffet.

③ Kintaro
MAP H2 ▪ 788 Denman St
▪ 604 682 7568 ▪ $

Expect lots of slurping at the counter of this no-frills *ramenya*, which is wildly popular for its BBQ pork *shio*.

④ Viet Sub
MAP K4 ▪ 520 Robson St ▪ 604 569 3340 ▪ $

Try Vietnamese favorites like shrimp salad rolls, pho, and lemongrass chicken at bargain prices.

⑤ Fujiya
MAP K3 ▪ 112-1050 W Pender St ▪ 604 608 1050 ▪ $

Made-to-order take-out sushi and the freshest sashimi is dished up here, and served either in individual bento boxes or on bigger sushi trays for large groups to share.

⑥ Bellaggio Café
MAP K3 ▪ 773 Hornby St ▪ 604 408 1281 ▪ $

Snag a booth in this stylish Italian restaurant, and be sure to ask about the daily pasta special, served with garlic bread. There's also a good choice of BC wines.

⑦ Pacific Centre Food Court

Choose from Japanese or Chinese made-to-order dishes, pizza, burgers, tacos, juices, sodas, ice creams or frozen yogurts in the wide (and child-friendly) selection of eateries that occupy the food court of this popular shopping mall (see p61).

⑧ The Gallery Café
MAP K3 ▪ 750 Hornby St ▪ 604 688 2233 ▪ $

Pick from a range of soups, salads, and sandwiches, then peruse the collections and exhibitions at the Vancouver Art Gallery (see pp20–21).

⑨ Pita Wrap Cafe
MAP K3 ▪ 565 Dunsmuir St
▪ 604 681 7634 ▪ $

Dine on Middle Eastern-style meat or vegetarian combos and falafel wraps at this tiny takeout. You'll need two hands to eat the wraps and plenty of napkins at the ready.

⑩ La Taqueria Pinche Taco Shop
MAP K3 ▪ 586 Hornby St ▪ 604 565 0511 ▪ $

Choose from authentic Mexican soft tacos, made with local and organic ingredients using traditional recipes, or sip on some *horchata* (sweet rice drink).

Restaurants

1 Gotham Steakhouse
MAP K3 ■ 615 Seymour St
■ 604 605 8282 ■ $$$
Indulge in the seafood tower filled with fresh crab, prawns, and oysters, or choose from the choicest steaks. End your meal with the bourbon cake.

2 Royal Dinette
MAP K3 ■ 905 Dunsmuir St
■ 604 974 8077 ■ $$
Chefs in the open kitchen push boundaries with creative local flavors, and there are great cocktails and craft beers to pair with the food.

3 Forage
Set in the Listel Hotel (see p116), this gathering spot for locavores is all about good sustainable dining and organic produce.

4 Diva at the Met
MAP K3 ■ Metropolitan Hotel, 645 Howe St ■ 604 602 7788 ■ $$
In the open kitchen, chefs conjure up gastronomical magic. An exceptional wine list includes BC wines (see p59).

5 YEW Seafood + Bar
MAP K3 ■ 791 W Georgia St
■ 604 692 4939 ■ $$
The focus is on Pacific Northwest seafood, but local chicken, lamb, and steak also make the cut (see p59).

6 Coast
MAP J3 ■ 1054 Alberni St ■ 604 685 5010 ■ $$
This vibrant place showcases BC's finest, freshest fish and seafood – try one of the seafood towers.

7 Le Crocodile
MAP J3 ■ 100-909 Durrard St
■ 604 669 4298 ■ $$$
Alsatian tart has been the signature dish at this elegant French restaurant

Paella brunch at Medina Café

PRICE CATEGORIES
For a three-course meal for one with half a bottle of wine (or equivalent meal), taxes, and extra charges.

$ under $35 $$ $35–85 $$$ over $85

for many years. The list of French wines here is extensive, and the service is impeccable.

8 Medina Café
MAP K4 ■ 780 Richards St
■ 604 879 3114 ■ $$
One of the best brunch spots in the city, which serves strong coffee and strong cocktails along with Mediterranean-style food – cassoulet, paella, or couscous.

9 Hawksworth
MAP K3 ■ 801 W Georgia St ■ 604 673 7000 ■ $$$
Contemporary cuisine is the order of the day at this restaurant (see p59) set in the Rosewood Hotel Georgia (see p116).

10 CinCin Ristorante & Bar
MAP J3 ■ 1154 Robson St
■ 604 688 7338 ■ $$$
Delicious rotisserie meats, risotto, and pasta are served in this Italian-themed restaurant popular with visiting Hollywood stars (see p59).

Terrace at CinCin Ristorante & Bar

See map on pp74–5

TOP10 South Granville and Yaletown

The neighborhoods of South Granville and Yaletown are separated by Granville Bridge and False Creek. On the south shore, South Granville offers a pleasant mix of upscale shops and restaurants. Granville Island is a bustling maze of converted warehouses overlooking False Creek, with a large public market as its centerpiece. Yaletown, on the north shore of the creek, began life as a railway works yard. Since the early 1990s, Yaletown has undergone a transformation, and the once-decrepit area now booms with condos, boutiques, bars, and restaurants.

Ship figurehead in the Vancouver Maritime Museum

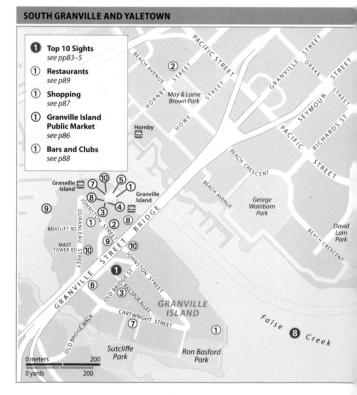

SOUTH GRANVILLE AND YALETOWN

1 **Top 10 Sights**
see pp83–5

1 **Restaurants**
see p89

1 **Shopping**
see p87

1 **Granville Island Public Market**
see p86

1 **Bars and Clubs**
see p88

Fishermen's Wharf, Granville Island

1 Granville Island

The original mudflats of False Creek were a fishing ground for the Squamish people. Industry moved in, polluting much of the turn-of-the-19th-century city. In the 1970s, that all changed with the redevelopment of Granville Island. Under the aegis of the federal government, heavy industry moved out and Granville Island quickly became a colorful, lively, bustling community (see pp24–5).

2 Sunset Beach
MAP H4

The white sands of Sunset Beach (see p47), which marks the end of English Bay and the start of False Creek, provide an ideal setting for swimming. Summer water temperatures rise to 65° F (18° C), and lifeguards are on duty from mid-May to Labour Day. The west end of Sunset Beach provides a good view of the gray granite Inukshuk (see p43). The Vancouver Aquatic Centre, at the east end of the beach, has an Olympic-size swimming pool. False Creek Ferries (see p111) dock behind the center.

Street in Yaletown Warehouse District

3 Yaletown Warehouse District
MAP J4–K5

Several warehouses have been transformed into lofts and stores, café terraces have sprung up on old loading docks, and high-rises have filled Yaletown's skyline. Along with the new residents has come a face-lift. Homer, Hamilton, and Mainland streets have been spruced up, making the most of heritage architectural features, including the red brick and arched doorways. Many brew pubs and nightclubs keep the area hopping at night.

YALETOWN'S RAILWAY HISTORY

Yaletown was first settled by Canadian Pacific Railway (CPR) train crews and laborers who arrived after the CPR closed its construction camp in Yale, BC, on completion of the transcontinental railway to Vancouver in 1887. In the early 1990s, Yaletown was the decaying heart of the city's industrial activity, when a development plan started its transformation into a lively urban area. In just over 20 years, Yaletown became the city's hottest community.

4 Vancouver Maritime Museum

MAP G4 ■ 1905 Ogden Ave ■ 604 257 8300 ■ Open 10am–5pm daily (to 8pm Thu) ■ Adm

Highlights of the West Coast's rich maritime history include seagoing canoes and a 1928 RCMP schooner, which was the first ship to circumnavigate North America. Kids can play with the discovery center's telescopes, computer games, and underwater robot (see p41).

5 H. R. MacMillan Space Centre

MAP G4 ■ 1100 Chestnut St ■ 604 738 7827 ■ Open daily (hours vary) ■ Adm

Space lore is presented in hands-on displays and multimedia shows here. A demonstration theater, and the Cosmic Courtyard's interactive gallery bring space to life. The Planetarium's multimedia shows feature space and astronomy inside a 65-ft (20-m) dome.

6 Roundhouse Arts & Recreation Centre

MAP K5 ■ 181 Roundhouse Mews ■ 604 713 1800 ■ www.round house.ca

Located on Beach Avenue in a former Canadian Pacific Railway switching building, the Roundhouse includes theater and gallery spaces and a host of community arts and athletic programs. It also houses the locomotive that pulled the first passenger train to Vancouver in 1887.

Locomotive 374 in the Roundhouse

7 Gallery Row

MAP H6 ■ 2100-2400 Granville St

Over a dozen art and antique galleries line the four-block stretch of Granville Street between 5th Avenue and West Broadway. There is no greater concentration of galleries in the city.

Vanier Park, with downtown Vancouver rising behind

8 False Creek
MAP J6–L5

As its name implies, False Creek is not a creek at all but a saltwater inlet. In the heart of the city, it extends east from Burrard Bridge to Science World. In the 1850s, Captain G. H. Richards sailed up this body of water, which then covered what is now Chinatown, eastward to Clark Drive, hoping to find the Fraser River. Disappointed, he named it False Creek. The mudflats Richards saw were fishing grounds for the Squamish people. Today, paved False Creek Seawall joins English Bay Seawall just east of Burrard Bridge and circles the creek. It's ideal for in-line skaters, cyclists, and walkers.

9 Museum of Vancouver
MAP G5 ▪ 1100 Chestnut St ▪ 604 736 4431 ▪ Open 10am–5pm daily (to 8pm Thu) ▪ Adm

Canada's largest civic museum boasts exhibits ranging from a fur-trading post to an amazing display of neon signs. Artifacts from a huge collection make up natural history, archaeology, Asian arts, and ethnology displays.

10 Vanier Park
MAP G4

This park is a calming oasis in the midst of the city. Boats sail by on English Bay, and pedestrians pass through on route to Kitsilano Beach or Granville Island. Coast Salish people once inhabited the park area. It is now home to the H. R. MacMillan Space Centre, Museum of Vancouver, and Vancouver Maritime Museum.

A DAY IN YALETOWN AND AT GRANVILLE ISLAND

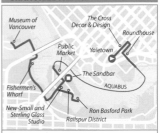

▶ MORNING

Start in **Yaletown Warehouse District** *(see p83)* at the corner of Drake and Hamilton streets for a 15-minute stroll north on Hamilton, noting its historic buildings. At Helmcken Street, turn right, then right again at Mainland Street. Spend half an hour in the shops, ending at **The Cross Decor & Design** *(see p87)*. Cross Pacific Boulevard to admire the **Roundhouse**'s locomotive 374. Take 15 minutes to explore the complex, then hop on the **Aquabus** *(see p111)* from the dock behind the center for the trip to **Granville Island** *(see pp24–5)*. For a fun hour, wander the **Public Market**, buying food for a casual lunch on a waterside bench.

AFTERNOON

Exit the market's east side. Continue on Johnston Street past Ocean Concrete. Turn right on Old Bridge Street to watch the glassblower at **New-Small and Sterling Glass Studio** *(see p24)*. Walk to **Railspur District**, on your left. Browse the shops for about 20 minutes, then cross Railspur Park to Cartwright Street. Turn left and walk to the end, to **Ron Basford Park**, where kids love running up "the mound." Back on Johnston Street, head west walking along the Seawall, passing by **Fishermen's Wharf** toward Vanier Park to find the large **Museum of Vancouver**, allowing yourself an hour there. End the day at **The Sandbar** *(see p89)* for some breathtaking views of the market, False Creek, and the city's West End.

See map on pp82–3 ←

Granville Island Public Market

1 International Food Courts
Two food courts offer sit-down and takeout food, including Indian, Mexican, Japanese, and Ukrainian. Patience may be required to land one of the limited indoor tables.

2 Stuart's Bakery
Mouthwatering pies, chocolate confections, and pastries fill one counter; multigrain, cheese, and other loaves crowd the other.

Fruit tart from Stuart's Bakery

3 JJ Bean
The Granville Island outlet was JJ Bean's very first coffee shop, which opened next to their roastery. The roast is full bodied and rich and all drinks are takeout – you can buy beans but there are no baked goods.

4 Olde World Fudge
Irresistible Belgian chocolate treats are concocted on-site in a copper vat. Assorted gift boxes include fudge, toffee, brittles, and caramel apples. Samples available.

5 Public Market Courtyard
On the east side of the market, enjoy tucking into your food as you take in the free entertainment in the open-air waterside Market Courtyard. The courtyard's worn floor planks from its days as an industrial dock only add to the charm.

6 Day Vendors
Specialty stalls sell an assortment of locally made wares, including seasonal and one-off items. Bowls made of BC wood, Thai curry sauces, herb seedlings, homemade pies, and jewelry are just the start. Vendors may not be located in the same place from day to day.

7 Granville Island Market Tour
Foodie Tours: 604 295 8844; www.foodietours.ca

If you're keen to get tastings from artisans across the market, sign up for a foodie market tour. Knowledgeable guides lead you to the very best local producers and you'll try cured meats, cheeses, donuts and fruit, among other delectable delights.

8 Lee's Donuts
Hailed as the best donut maker on the West Coast, this Granville Island institution (it's been here since 1979) serves the lightest, fluffiest donuts you will ever taste, and you can watch them being made.

9 Marina
At the marina on the market's west side you'll find fancy yachts, sail boats, and the occasional fishing boat. Tall ships dock here during festivals.

10 Public Market Building
At Granville Island's west end is the large Public Market, partly housed in a wood-frame, corrugated tin-clad warehouse. Built in the early 1920s by the Island's first tenant, BC Equipment, this structure set the architectural style of the Island. The timbered beams and massive pulleys and hooks once pulled rope coils from one area to the other.

Exterior of the Public Market Building

Shopping

Wood crafts at the Circle Craft Co-op

1 Circle Craft Co-op
MAP H5 ■ 1666 Johnston St
■ 604 669 8021

The best of BC crafts, from handmade clothing to one-of-a-kind jewelry. There's also wall art, wood crafts ceramics, and hand-blown glass.

2 Meinhardts
MAP B2 ■ 3002 Granville St
■ 604 732 4405

This iconic south Granville food emporium has a similar design to NYC's famous Dean & DeLuca and is based around the concept of buying fresh ingredients on a regular basis.

3 The Cross Decor & Design
MAP J5 ■ 1198 Homer St ■ 604 689 2900

Located in a 1914 heritage building, this fabulous store sources items from all over the world, and also features pieces by local artists and vendors.

4 Lussobaby
MAP B2 ■ 2699 Granville St
■ 604 736 0648

This store has toys and clothing for babies and kids, including locally made items that make great gifts.

5 Karameller Candy Shop
MAP K5 ■ 1020 Mainland St
■ 604 639 0325

This shop stocks rows of Swedish candies and chocolates made without high-fructose corn syrup.

6 Town Shoes
MAP B2 ■ 2867 Granville St
■ 604 732 5011

Since 1952 this largest branded Canadian footwear store has been selling stylish footwear, from Birkenstocks to Nine West heels.

7 Forge and Form
MAP H6 ■ 1334 Cartwright St
■ 604 684 6298

High-end gold and silver jewelry with precious stones. Choose from bold rings and pretty, fluid necklaces.

8 Swirl Wine Store
MAP K5 ■ 1185 Mainland St
■ 604 408 9463

This shop sells the best selection of BC wines at vineyard prices, as well as gourmet gift baskets. They also have free wine-tasting sessions.

Tasting at Swirl Wine Store

9 Boboli
MAP B2 ■ 2776 Granville St
■ 604 257 2300

Trend setting styles from a variety of men's and women's lines, including Missoni, Etro, and Blumarine.

10 Malaspina Printmakers Gallery
MAP H5 ■ 1555 Duranleau St ■ 604 688 1724

Prints by Canadian (particularly BC) and international artists with images and styles to suit all tastes.

See map on pp82–3 ←

Bars and Clubs

Dockside Restaurant and Brewing Company

1 Dockside Restaurant and Brewing Company

This popular bar is located in the Granville Island Hotel (see p117). Savor the delicious beer brewed here while admiring the boats on False Creek from the fantastic patio area.

2 Long Table Distillery
MAP K3 ■ 1451 Hornby St ■ 604 266 0177

This is the first micro-distillery of the city, crafting small-batch gin and premium spirits. Enjoy the light snacks and cocktails on weekends.

3 The Liberty Distillery
MAP H5 ■ 1494 Old Bridge St ■ 604 558 1998

Only BC-grown grains and ingredients go into the spirits here, which are fermented and distilled on-site in handmade copper stills. Book a tour or pop into the lounge for a cocktail.

Cocktail at the Liberty Distillery

4 Yaletown Brewing Company
MAP K5 ■ 1111 Mainland St ■ 604 681 2739

Choose from the extensive selection of locally brewed beer here while dining on some excellent homestyle cooking in the pub, the restaurant, or out on the popular patio.

5 The New Oxford
MAP K5 ■ 1144 Homer St ■ 604 609 0901

A 50-ft- (15-m-) long bar is the centerpiece at this tongue-in-cheek nod to Oxford University and British sporting culture.

6 Granville Island Brewing

Established in 1984, the brewery is the place to buy bottles, get your growler refilled, or reserve a keg for an event. They organize tours and tastings, but you'll get a warm welcome in the laidback industrial-feel taproom too (see pp24–5).

7 The Refinery
MAP J4 ■ 1115 Granville St ■ 604 687 8001

This new-world eatery and bar with an old-world atmosphere attracts sustainability-conscious diners and experienced cocktailers alike.

8 Backstage Lounge
MAP H5 ■ 1585 Johnston St ■ 604 687 1354

This low-key hangout attracts theatergoers and actors from the Granville Island Stage next door. Live music is performed, with a focus on local talent.

9 Opus Bar
MAP K5 ■ 350 Davie St ■ 604 642 6787

This sophisticated hotel bar attracts a chic crowd. Happy hour is from 3–6pm daily, with $5 drinks and snacks.

10 Bar None
MAP J5 ■ 1222 Hamilton St ■ 604 689 7000

In a converted warehouse, this New York-style nightclub draws a hip crowd. There is live music, a spacious dance floor, and ample seating.

See map on pp82–3

Restaurants

PRICE CATEGORIES
For a three-course meal for one with half a bottle of wine (or equivalent meal), taxes, and extra charges.

$ under $35 $$ $35–85 $$$ over $85

1 Blue Water Café
MAP K4 ▪ 1095 Hamilton St ▪ 604 688 8078 ▪ $$

On offer are masterfully prepared West Coast dishes made with the freshest local fish, plus sushi made with coastal shellfish *(see p58)*.

2 Rodney's Oyster House
MAP J5 ▪ 1228 Hamilton St ▪ 604 609 0080 ▪ $$

The action is at the counter, so sidle up and order any of the many oyster types on offer, shucked as you watch. Steamed clams and mussels, crab, and Atlantic lobster are also featured.

3 Cioppino's Mediterranean Grill
MAP J5 ▪ 1133 Hamilton St ▪ 604 688 7466 ▪ $$

Chef "Pino" Posteraro creates lighter versions of traditional Italian pasta, risottos, and seafood *(see p59)*.

4 West
MAP B2 ▪ 2881 Granville St ▪ 604 738 8938 ▪ $$$

Vancouver's perennial favorite serves contemporary regional cuisine, prepared with seasonal ingredients, and boasts of an award-winning wine list.

Stylish interior of West

5 Provence Marinaside
MAP K5 ▪ 1177 Marinaside Cres ▪ 604 681 4144 ▪ $$

This pretty restaurant and bar has a sommelier to help select wine, and picnic baskets are available.

6 The Flying Pig
MAP J5 ▪ 1168 Hamilton St ▪ 604 568 1344 ▪ $$

With a casual setting, this restaurant serves innovative Canadian cuisine. Try the classic poutine with pork.

7 Small Victory Bakery
MAP K4 ▪ 1088 Homer St ▪ 604 899 8892 ▪ $

A modern café that offers wonderful croissants and cakes, as well as light breakfast and lunch snacks.

8 Brix & Mortar
MAP K5 ▪ 1138 Homer St ▪ 604 915 9463 ▪ $$

Set in a 1912 heritage building, this wine and tapas bar has excellent set menus featuring West Coast cuisine.

9 Edible Canada
MAP H5 ▪ 1596 Johnston St ▪ 604 682 6681 ▪ $$

A casual bistro that serves Canadian cuisine made with locally sourced organic ingredients.

10 The Sandbar
MAP H5 ▪ 1535 Johnston St ▪ 604 669 9030 ▪ $$

Feast on Dungeness crab cakes and cedar-planked salmon while enjoying breathtaking views of False Creek.

TOP10 Vancouver Island

A world away from buzzing Vancouver, but easily accessible by ferry or seaplane, picturesque Vancouver Island is where city folk go for downtime. Located at the very south of the island, the provincial capital Victoria is the first stop for most visitors. The rest of the sparsely populated island offers protected parkland, endless beaches, offshore islets, and fishing villages.

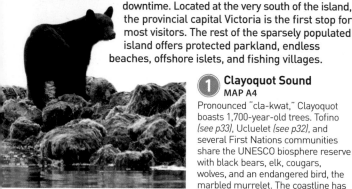

Black bear in Clayoquot Sound

1 Clayoquot Sound
MAP A4

Pronounced "cla-kwat," Clayoquot boasts 1,700-year-old trees. Tofino (see p33), Ucluelet (see p32), and several First Nations communities share the UNESCO biosphere reserve with black bears, elk, cougars, wolves, and an endangered bird, the marbled murrelet. The coastline has bays, intertidal lagoons, and mudflats.

VANCOUVER ISLAND

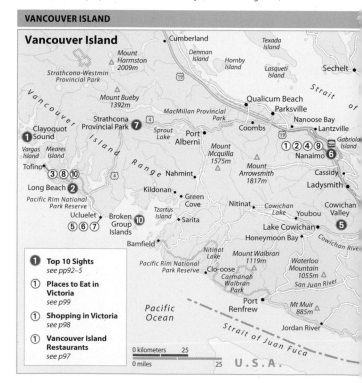

Vancouver Island

- Cumberland
- Texada Island
- Mount Harmston 2009m
- Denman Island
- Hornby Island
- Lasqueti Island
- Sechelt
- Strathcona-Westmin Provincial Park
- Mount Bueby 1392m
- MacMillan Provincial Park
- Qualicum Beach
- Parksville
- Strait
- **7** Strathcona Provincial Park
- Sprout Lake
- Coombs
- Nanoose Bay
- Lantzville
- of
- **1** Clayoquot Sound
- Port Alberni
- **1 2 4 9**
- Gabriola Island
- Vargas Island
- Meares Island
- Mount Mcquilla 1575m
- Nanaimo **6**
- Tofino **3 8 10**
- Nahmint
- Mount Arrowsmith 1817m
- Cassidy
- Long Beach **2**
- Kildonan
- Ladysmith
- Pacific Rim National Park Reserve
- Green Cove
- Nitinat
- Cowichan Lake
- Cowichan Valley
- Ucluelet **5 6 7**
- Tzartus Island
- Youbou
- Broken Group Islands **10**
- Sarita
- Lake Cowichan
- **5**
- Bamfield
- Honeymoon Bay
- Cowichan River
- Nitinat Lake
- Mount Walbran 1119m
- Waterloo Mountain 1055m
- Pacific Rim National Park Reserve
- Clo-oose
- Carmanah Walbran Park
- San Juan River
- **Pacific Ocean**
- Port Renfrew
- Mt Muir 885m
- Jordan River
- Strait of Juan de Fuca
- 0 kilometers 25
- 0 miles 25
- U.S.A.

1 Top 10 Sights
see pp92–5

1 Places to Eat in Victoria
see p99

1 Shopping in Victoria
see p98

1 Vancouver Island Restaurants
see p97

Previous pages Sunset over Georgia Strait from a beach in Nanaimo

Shoreline of Long Beach after a sunset, Pacific Rim National Park

② Long Beach

The 16-km (10-mile) stretch of coastline located between Tofino (see p33) and Ucluelet (see p32) is part of the Pacific Rim National Park Reserve of Canada. Backed by forests and with wide vistas of the wild Pacific Ocean, the beach is a must-see. Visitors can hike, surf, and learn about the Nuu-chah-nulth peoples, whose home this has been for centuries (see pp32–3).

③ Gulf Islands
MAP E5

Visitors flock to these islands in the Strait of Georgia. Salt Spring, with its many artists' studios, and Galiano, which has a lovely provincial park, are the most popular island destinations. Saturna, Pender, Mayne, and Gabriola are the other major islands. Each has its own personality; all are accessible by ferry from Swartz Bay (see p114).

Stream at Goldstream Provincial Park

④ Goldstream Provincial Park

MAP E6 ■ Visitor Centre: 2930 Trans Canada Hwy; 250 478 9414; open 9am–4:30pm daily

Massive old-growth Douglas firs tower overhead in this mystic rain forest only 12 miles (19 km) from Victoria. The park's waterfall drops 155 ft (48 m) into a canyon pool and is easily reached by foot. An annual fall salmon run on the Goldstream River attracts hundreds of majestic bald eagles. Once a fishing ground for the Coast Salish, the park was overrun by miners during the Gold Rush of the 1850s (see p38). A visitor centre provides information on the park.

⑤ Cowichan Valley

MAP D5

This pastoral valley is a mix of forests and farmland. Its wines, ciders, and gourmet cheeses attract foodies from miles around. Cowichan Lake is Vancouver Island's main freshwater lake and a terrific spot for swimming, canoeing, and fishing. The Cowichan River is also famed for its fly-fishing.

DUNCAN, THE CITY OF TOTEMS

The world's largest outdoor collection of totem poles can be explored in Duncan, a city on the traditional lands of the Cowichan First Nation in the Cowichan Valley. Carved in western red cedar, the poles bear designs represent family crests and traditional symbols in Coast Salish and Kwakwaka'wakw culture, and were once a record of significant events.

⑥ Nanaimo

MAP D4 ■ The Bastion: 98 Front St; open 10am–5pm; adm; www.nanaimomuseum.ca

The Old Quarter, built when Nanaimo was a coal-mining town, boasts many 19th-century buildings, including the 1895 Nanaimo Court House. Stroll along the Harbourfront Walkway, stopping at The Bastion Nanaimo Museum. Nanaimo Downtown Farmers' Market is held next to The Bastion on Fridays (May–Oct).

⑦ Strathcona Provincial Park

www.env.gov.bc.ca

This vast area of rugged mountain wilderness in the interior of Vancouver Island has been a provincial park since 1911. Snowy peaks make a stunning backdrop to the park's many hiking trails; at 7,218 ft (2,200 m) the Golden Hinde dominates the south of the island. Buttle Lake is the largest body of water in the park and is a popular place to set up camp.

⑧ Butchart Gardens

MAP E5 ■ 800 Benvenuto Ave, Brentwood Bay ■ 250 652 5256 ■ Open daily ■ Adm

For over a century, the incomparable Butchart Gardens, wrung out of a worked-out quarry, have awed visitors with their lush beauty (see p44).

Sunken garden at Butchart Gardens

⑨ Victoria

With outstanding historic and cultural sights, including the Royal British Columbia Museum, Emily Carr's House, and the Art Gallery of Greater Victoria, the provincial capital *(see pp28–9)* makes a pleasant base for visits to Vancouver Island. A mild climate, lovely parks and gardens, and great vistas from the Inner Harbour add to the city's charm. The waters around Victoria are also a great spot for whale-watching, especially between May and November.

Sea kayaking around Barkley Sound

⑩ Broken Group Islands
MAP B5

An archipelago of some 100 rugged islands and islets is a paradise for nature lovers, kayakers, and scuba divers. The area around Barkley Sound has outstanding views of coastal rain forest, beaches, and sea caves. Accessible only by boat, this isolated wilderness is best experienced via a guided tour.

WALKING TOUR OF VICTORIA

▶ MORNING

Starting at the corner of Wharf Street and Douglas Street visit the **Maritime Museum of British Columbia** *(see p29)* and devote an hour to its displays before heading north on Government Street. At Fisgard Street, the colorful Chinese-style Gate of **Harmonious** Interest welcomes you to **Chinatown** *(see p29)*. Explore the area for an hour, dipping into tiny **Fan Tan Alley**, off Fisgard Street. Continue south to **Bastion Square**, the heart of Old Town, where fur traders boozed and brawled in the days of Fort Victoria. Head to the **Irish Times Pub** *(1200 Government Street; open 7am–1am daily)* for tasty fish and chips.

AFTERNOON

Admire the marine traffic from the **Inner Harbour** *(see p28)*. At the far end of the harbor, cross Belleville Street to the statue of a youthful Queen Victoria by the **BC Parliament Buildings** *(see pp28–9)*. The fascinating **Royal British Columbia Museum** *(see pp28–9)* next door will take about two hours to peruse. Exit the museum on the east side to admire the fascinating totem poles in **Thunderbird Park** *(see p30)* before checking out the historic **Hulmcken House** *(see p31)* nearby. Cross Belleville Street to the **Fairmont Empress Hotel** *(see p119)* for a glimpse of the grand lobby. Have dinner at **Red Fish Blue Fish** *(see p99)* on Broughton Street Pier to replenish your energy.

See map on pp92–3

Outdoor Activities

① Rock Climbing
Strathcona Park Lodge: 41040 Gold River Hwy, Campbell River, 250 286 3122; www.strathconapark lodge.com

Climbers can explore any one of the three bluffs and view the vistas across Upper Campbell Lake, with the guided tours of Strathcona Park Lodge.

② Fishing
Both fly-fishing and salmon fishing are popular. The action-packed east coast Campbell River, known as "the salmon capital of the world," is a highlight February through to March.

③ Hiking
Hikers gravitate to the west coast for the summer-only West Coast Trail *(see p33)*. Just as scenic, but shorter, are the Juan de Fuca Marine Trail and Wild Pacific Trail.

④ Skiing
Mount Washington Alpine Resort: www.mountwashington.ca

Mount Washington has some of the best powder in BC to ski, snowboard, cross-country, and toboggan.

⑤ Camping
Picturesque campgrounds are scattered across Vancouver Island and the Gulf Islands. Hello BC *(see p115)*, the BC tourism website, has comprehensive listings.

Scenic camping in the snow

Kayaking in the Strait of Georgia

⑥ Kayaking and Canoeing
Ocean River Sports: 250 381 4233; www.oceanriver.com

For ocean paddling there's the Broken Group Islands, Clayoquot Sound, the Gulf Islands, and Nanaimo. If you like lakes, explore Elk and Beaver Lake. Hire equipment at Ocean River Sports.

⑦ Diving
Sink or Swim Scuba: 250 758 7946; www.scubananaimo.ca

Winter diving is best for visibility. Popular dive spots include Barkley Sound, Browning Wall, Discovery, and wrecks off the coast near Nanaimo. Sink or Swim Scuba offers equipment hire and PADI courses.

⑧ Biking
From gentle cycling in Victoria to serious off-road mountain biking in the Comox Valley, Vancouver Island has something for everyone. There is a good choice of tour and rental companies *(see p111)*.

⑨ Surfing
Pacific Surf School: 250 725 2155 ■ Surf Sister Surf School: 250 725 4456

Access to the wild west coast and the Pacific Ocean make surfing popular on Vancouver Island, especially in Tofino and Long Beach. Chesterman Beach is a great place for beginners.

⑩ Whale-Watching
Between April and October, you can spot resident orcas (killer whales). In May, June, September and October, migratory humpback whales pass the BC coast, and gray whales *(see p32)* do so in spring. You can see minke whales all year round.

Vancouver Island Restaurants

1 Hilltop Bistro
5281 Rutherford Rd, Nanaimo
■ 250 585 5337 ■ $$

This intimate and rustic bistro served nose-to-tail cooking before it was trendy, and it continues to focus on seasonal produce and great service.

2 Nori Japanese Restaurant
6750 Island Hwy, Unit 203, Nanaimo
■ 250 751 3377 ■ $

The location of this award-winning restaurant might not inspire (it's set on the highway), but the sushi and sashimi are the best in town.

PRICE CATEGORIES
For a three-course meal for one with half a bottle of wine (or equivalent meal), taxes, and extra charges.

$ under $35 $$ $35–85 $$$ over $85

6 Hank's Untraditional BBQ
1576 Imperial Ln, Ucluelet ■ 250 726 2225 ■ $$

The is the number one place to fill up on smoked and slow-cooked meats. It is relaxed and casual, with big meaty portions, friendly service, and local beers on tap.

7 Norwoods
1714 Peninsula Rd, Ucluelet ■ 250 726 7001 ■ $$

This fine-dining place with an outdoor terrace is known for its wine-bar feel. There are plenty of seafood options and everything is seasonal and cooked to perfection.

Dinner with a view at the Pointe Restaurant

3 The Pointe Restaurant
Wickaninnish Inn, 500 Osprey Ln, Tofino ■ 250 725 3100 ■ $$$

This restaurant has panoramic views of the wild Pacific Ocean and a great fine-dining menu. Try the weekly tasting menu paired with BC wines.

4 Bee's Knees Café
208 Wallace St, Nanaimo
■ 250 591 5250 ■ $

This cozy community café has a limited menu, which changes daily, but the great coffee is a staple.

5 Zoe's Bakery and Café
250 Main St, Ucluelet ■ 250 726 2253 ■ $

Equally loved by locals and visitors alike, Zoe's Bakery is a wholefoods bakery that is proudly pro-gluten (and definitely pro-butter).

8 Common Loaf
180 First St, Tofino
■ 250 725 3915 ■ $

An institution in Tofino, this quirky cash-only bakeshop has provided the town with artisan breads and sweet baked goods for years.

9 Gabriel's Gourmet Café
39A Commercial St, Nanaimo
■ 250 714 0271 ■ $

Set right in the heart of Nanaimo is Gabriel's, who can tell you where they've sourced every ingredient. The popular brunch is served until 3pm.

10 Chocolate Tofino
1180 A Pacific Rim Hwy, Tofino
■ 250 725 2526

Exquisite handcrafted chocolate gelato and sorbet are served in this tiny shack – you can even watch the chocolatiers at work. There are long lines for the gelato in summer.

See map on pp92–3

Shopping in Victoria

Items for sale in Fort Street Antiques

1 Fort Street Antiques
MAP Q3 ■ Fort St between Douglas St & Cook St

Discover one-of-a-kind silverware, glass and china, fine art, furniture, and jewelry on upper Fort Street.

2 WIN Pandora
MAP Q2 ■ 785 Pandora Ave ■ 250 480 4006

Victoria's community cooperative Women In Need (WIN) has several secondhand boutiques dotted around the city; Pandora is a great place to find vintage clothing and accessories.

3 Bernstein & Gold
MAP P2 ■ 608 Yates St ■ 250 384 7899

Head to this lifestyle boutique for carefully chosen homewares, jewelry, footwear, and leather goods, as well as great skin-care brands and a spa.

4 Silk Road Tea
MAP P1 ■ 1624 Government St ■ 250 382 0006

Silk Road offers a tea-tasting bar similar to a wine bar. In addition to tea, it has a spa *(see p48)* and its own line of natural body-care products.

5 She She Bags
MAP P2 ■ 616 View St ■ 250 388 0613

This place is purse heaven: from glitzy clutch bags to industrial laptop bags, this store has a bag for everyone.

6 Reunion Boutique
MAP P2 ■ 585 Johnson St ■ 250 380 0906

At this unisex boutique, mod meets boho-chic. There's great clothing by both international designers and homegrown talent.

7 Fan Tan Home & Style
MAP P1 ■ 541 Fisgard St ■ 250 382 4424

This store sells gifts from around the world, with a focus on India, Indonesia, China, and France. Home accessories include mats, art, baskets, linens, and curios.

8 Violette Boutique
MAP P2 ■ 1303 Government St ■ 250 388 7752

Inspired by Paris jewelry boutiques, the owner stocks mainly Canadian-made pieces, both dainty and chunky.

9 Capital Iron
MAP E6 ■ 1900 Store St ■ 250 385 9703

Opened since 1934, this iconic hardware store sells great outdoor clothing and gear.

10 Munro's Books
MAP P2 ■ 1108 Government St ■ 250 382 2464

A fantastic bookstore founded by Jim Munro and his wife, Alice Munro, the Noble Prize-winning author.

Exterior of Munro's Books

Places to Eat in Victoria

1 Fairmont Empress Hotel
A variety of colonial-themed dining venues await at Victoria's grandest hotel *(see p119)*. Especially popular is the formal afternoon tea, served daily since 1908 – advance reservations are required.

PRICE CATEGORIES

For a three-course meal for one with half a bottle of wine (or equivalent meal), taxes, and extra charges.

$ under $35   **$$** $35–85   **$$$** over $85

Inside the Fairmont Empress Hotel

2 Olo
MAP P1 ■ 509 Fisgard St ■ 250 590 8795 ■ $$

A small restaurant on the edge of Chinatown, this serves impeccable West Coast cuisine made with all local ingredients.

3 Spinnakers Gastro Brewpub
MAP E6 ■ 308 Catherine St, Victoria ■ 250 386 2739 ■ $$

Canada's oldest licensed brewpub serves all-natural smoked meats and sausages, perfect companions to the assortment of beers on tap.

4 Canoe
MAP N1 ■ 450 Swift St ■ 250 361 1940 ■ $$

Local organic produce, meat, and wild seafood are on offer at this brewpub, marina, and restaurant, in a historic 1894 waterfront property.

5 Brasserie L'École
MAP P1 ■ 1715 Government St ■ 250 475 6260 ■ $$

This place dishes up French bistro classics – lamb shank, mussels, and *frites* – made using local products.

6 Red Fish Blue Fish
MAP N3 ■ 1006 Wharf St ■ 250 298 6877 ■ $

Set in a shipping container on the Inner Harbour, this seasonal canteen-style fish restaurant serves sustainable seafood.

7 Il Terrazzo Ristorante
MAP P2 ■ 555 Johnson St ■ 250 361 0028 ■ $$

Enjoy fine Northern Italian food in the heated courtyard here. Wood-oven-roasted meats and pizzas, pastas, and seafood arrive with a flourish.

8 Pagliacci's
MAP P3 ■ 1011 Broad St ■ 250 386 1662 ■ $$

Linguine, lasagna, and fettuccine are simple and satisfying at this Italian place. Don't miss the Pag's bread.

9 The Noodle Box
MAP P3 ■ 818 Douglas St ■ 250 384 1314 ■ $

Huge portions of noodle and rice dishes come in decorative boxes here, and there are five levels of spiciness to suit every taste.

10 Wildfire Bakery
MAP E6 ■ 1517 Quadra St, Victoria ■ 250 383 3473 ■ $

This family-owned organic bakery and café offers artisan breads, cakes, and pastries, with wholesome savouries for breakfast and lunch.

See map on pp92–3

🔟 Greater Vancouver and Beyond

One of the reasons Vancouver is often listed as one of the world's best places to live is the wide range of things to do, and the breathtaking scenery in which to do them, just a short drive away from downtown. The ski slopes and golf courses of Whistler are reached after a scenic two-hour drive, ideal for an overnight excursion. Superb rain forests can be enjoyed in the west side of Vancouver's Pacific Spirit Regional Park and in North Vancouver's Capilano Suspension Bridge Park. Towns like Squamish or the community of Brackendale provide unforgettable nature walks, hikes, and climbs. Small waterfront towns such as Steveston, a former fishing village, have proudly preserved their local history.

Exhibit at the Museum of Anthropology at UBC

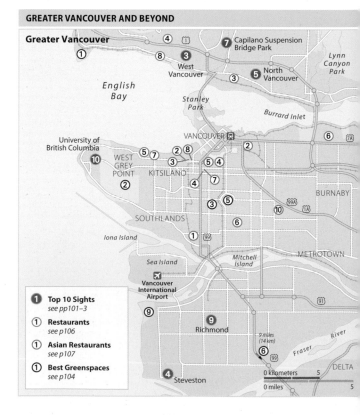

GREATER VANCOUVER AND BEYOND

Greater Vancouver

Capilano Suspension Bridge Park

Lynn Canyon Park

West Vancouver

North Vancouver

English Bay

Stanley Park

Burrard Inlet

VANCOUVER

University of British Columbia

WEST GREY POINT

KITSILANO

BURNABY

SOUTHLANDS

Iona Island

METROTOWN

Sea Island

Mitchell Island

✈ Vancouver International Airport

1 **Top 10 Sights**
see pp101–3

1 **Restaurants**
see p106

1 **Asian Restaurants**
see p107

1 **Best Greenspaces**
see p104

Richmond

9 miles (14 km)

Fraser River

DELTA

Steveston

0 kilometers   5

0 miles   5

Blackcomb Mountain and Harmony Lake in Whistler

1 Whistler

Two mountains, Whistler and Blackcomb, rise side by side at the popular resort town of Whistler. Ski in winter, enjoy views of the four villages and surrounding mountains and valleys from gondolas and lift chairs year-round, or cycle the Valley Trail in summer *(see pp34–5)*.

2 Grouse Mountain

MAP F3 ■ Visitor Centre: 6400 Nancy Greene Way, North Vancouver; 604 984 0661; www.grousemountain. com ■ Adm to Skyride

There's lots to do atop this Vancouver landmark. The Feasthouse invites visitors into a beautifully crafted cedar longhouse to learn about Pacific Northwest First Nations cultures. At night, legends come alive with local cuisine, song, and dance.

3 West Vancouver

MAP B1

Lighthouse Park *(see p47)*, Cypress Provincial Park *(see p104)*, and Horseshoe Bay are among the attractions here. A pleasant day-trip destination, Horseshoe Bay has a small bayside park with two totems. BC Ferries *(see p111)* depart here for Nanaimo, Bowen Island, and the Sunshine Coast. The pedestrian Centennial Seawall links Ambleside Park and the charming Dundarave village.

Point Atkinson Lighthouse in Lighthouse Park

North to Whistler

0 km 15
0 miles 15

Whistler
McGuire
Garibaldi Provincial Park
Garibaldi
△ *Mount Garibaldi 2636m*

BRITISH COLUMBIA

Garibaldi Highlands
Brackendale
Woodfibre
Squamish
Pitt River
Britannia Beach
Pinecone Burke Provincial Park
Ashlu River
Indian River
Anvil Island
Gambier Island
Brunswick
New Brighton
Lions Bay
Obelisk Peak 1655m
Grouse Mountain
Snug Cove
Bowen Island
VANCOUVER
Coquitlam
see map left
Surrey

Gulf of Georgia Cannery National Historic Site by the Fraser River, Steveston

4 Steveston

MAP B3 ■ Gulf of Georgia Cannery: 12138 4th Ave; 604 664 9009; open 10am–5pm daily; adm

Old-fashioned Steveston village was built on the salmon industry, with 15 canneries once employing thousands. The Gulf of Georgia Cannery National Historic Site offers a peek into this past. The converted 1894 building rests on pylons over the Fraser River. View the film inside, then tour the huge building. A children's discovery area is set up in the Ice House.

5 North Vancouver

MAP B1 ■ Lynn Canyon Park: at the end of Peters Rd, Lynn Valley ■ Lynn Canyon Ecology Centre: 604 990 3755

North Vancouver is a busy North Shore city of more than 53,000 residents. Take the scenic SeaBus ride across Burrard Inlet. Disembark at Lonsdale Quay, a public market selling fresh produce. To the east, Lynn Canyon Park boasts its own suspension bridge, spanning the dramatic canyon, 165 ft (50 m) above Lynn Creek, as well as 40 types of moss and 100-year-old Douglas firs. Stop in at the Ecology Centre to view the displays and films, and get details on park tours and trails.

6 Squamish

MAP E3

"Squamish," a Coast Salish word meaning "mother of the wind," is an apt name for this windy town that has become a major center for outdoor activities. Rock climbers relish the challenge of the Stawamus Chief, an imposing granite monolith. Others windsurf on the Squamish River or camp in nearby parks, including the renowned Garibaldi Provincial Park.

Windsurfing in Squamish

A CONVOCATION OF EAGLES

Almost half the world's bald eagle population lives in BC. Thousands make their annual winter home in Brackendale. The first eagle count took place along the Squamish River in 1985, when six people counted 500 eagles. Some 600 to 900 eagles are now counted annually. Brackendale Eagle Festival takes place every January.

Capilano Suspension Bridge Park

This North Vancouver park has been around since 1888. Its suspension bridge sways 230 ft (70 m) above the Capilano River (see pp16–17).

Brackendale
MAP E2

The community is best known for the bald eagles that winter in the nearby 3-sq-mile (7.8-sq-km) Brackendale Eagles Provincial Park, but the ocean and river location here make this small town a very popular place for rafting and canoeing.

Juvenile bald eagle in Brackendale

Richmond
MAP B3 ■ www.richmondnight market.com

BC's fourth-largest city is making waves as a multicultural foodie destination. The Richmond Night Market from May till October, and the International Buddhist Temple (see p63) are well worth traveling for.

University of British Columbia

MAP A2 ■ 604 822 2211 ■ www.ubc. ca ■ Gardens: open daily; 604 822 4208; www.botanicalgarden.ubc.ca; adm

A lovely mix of historic and modern architecture, the buildings of BC's oldest university are complemented by diverse gardens. Stroll around the traditional Japanese Nitobe Memorial Garden, or navigate suspended walkways high up in the tree canopy at the Botanical Garden.

A DRIVE ALONG THE SEA-TO-SKY HIGHWAY

 MORNING

Start your day heading north from **Vancouver** on the Sea-to-Sky Highway, which is officially known as Highway 99. Tiny **Britannia Beach** and its **Mine Museum** make an interesting first stop. **Shannon Falls**, just 4.5 miles (7 km) further on, is well worth the ten minutes on foot from the parking area off the highway. Continue driving on the dramatic coastal road to **Squamish** and take the ten-minute Sea-to-Sky Gondola to access summit trails, a suspension bridge, and beautiful, sweeping views. Have lunch at one of the three family-friendly eateries at Summit Lodge, 2,900 ft (885 m) above Howe Sound.

AFTERNOON

After lunch, continue your journey north toward **Whistler**. Make sure to leave time for the renowned **Garibaldi Provincial Park** and its namesake turquoise lake; there are five access points to the park between Squamish and Pemberton, all with parking for various trailheads. A short final drive through classic BC backcountry brings you to **Whistler** and the famous **Whistler Blackcomb** ski resort (see p105), where you can spend as many hours or days as your itinerary allows. Book relaxing spa treatments at **Scandinave** (see p49) or take to one of the championship golf courses found nearby. An indulgent dinner at the excellent **Trattoria di Umberto** restaurant (see p106) will make a perfect end to your day.

See map on pp100–101 ←

Best Greenspaces

1 Lighthouse Park
MAP A1 ▪ Marine Dr & Beacon Ln, West Vancouver ▪ 604 925 7275 ▪ www.westvancouver.ca

Giant ferns and huge boulders are signatures of this waterfront park. Quiet trails lead through the area's last stand of old-growth trees.

2 Pacific Spirit Regional Park
MAP A2 ▪ W 16th Ave at Blanca St ▪ 604 224 5739 ▪ www.metrovancouver.org

This huge park has over 45 miles (73 km) of trails through thick rain forest and along bogs and cliffs.

3 VanDusen Botanical Garden
MAP B2 ▪ 5151 Oak St ▪ 604 257 8335 ▪ Adm ▪ www.vandusengarden.org

Secluded nooks and crannies can still be found at this world-famous garden with seasonal flower displays.

4 Cypress Provincial Park
MAP E3 ▪ Top of Cypress Bowl Rd, West Vancouver ▪ 604 926 5612 ▪ www.cypressmountain.com

Cypress Mountain, in the park, offers sports galore and great views as far as Mount Baker in Washington State.

5 Queen Elizabeth Park
MAP B2 ▪ W 33rd Ave & Cambie St ▪ 311 ▪ www.vancouver.ca

This park, at the highest point in Vancouver, 499 ft (152 m) above sea level, offers a conservatory, lovely gardens, and splendid views (see p45).

6 Boundary Bay Regional Park
MAP F4 ▪ Boundary Bay Rd, Tsawwassen ▪ 604 224 5739 ▪ www.metrovancouver.org

This oceanside park is frequented by beachcombers, horseback riders, and birders throughout the year.

7 Mount Seymour Provincial Park
MAP C1 ▪ 1700 Mt Seymour Rd, North Vancouver ▪ 604 986 2261 ▪ www.mtseymour.ca

Mountaineers and skiers relish the snow and gentle slopes in winter. In summer, hikers come for the views.

8 George C. Reifel Migratory Bird Sanctuary
MAP E4 ▪ 5191 Robertson Rd ▪ 604 946 6980 ▪ Adm ▪ www.reifelbirdsanctuary.com

Some 60,000 birds visit this huge site on Westham Island yearly. View the wetlands from platforms and hides.

9 West Dyke Recreational Trail
MAP A3 ▪ www.richmond.ca

This 3.5-mile (5.5-km) trail offers views of Sturgeon Banks, which attracts 1.4 million birds annually.

10 Deer Lake Park
MAP C2 ▪ Canada Way & Sperling Ave, Burnaby ▪ 604 294 7450 ▪ www.burnaby.ca

This park has plenty of wildlife, trails, picnic spots, a playground, various art centers, a restaurant, and the open-air Burnaby Village Museum.

Conservatory at Queen Elizabeth Park

Adventure Sports

Mountain biking in Squamish

1 Mountain Biking
Mountain Biking BC: www.
mountainbikingbc.ca
The 93-mile (150-km) Sea-to-Sky
trail stretches from Squamish to
D'Arcy. Find trail maps on Mountain
Biking BC's website.

2 Heli-Snowboarding & Skiing
Whistler Heli-Skiing: 604 905 3337;
www.whistlerheliskiing.com
Fly away via helicopter from the
Whistler Blackcomb crowds into
the pristine high-alpine powder.

3 Kayaking with Orcas
Ecomarine Paddlesport Centres:
604 689 7575; www.ecomarine.com
Paddle alongside an orca pod at
Vancouver Island's spectacular
glacier-carved eastern coastline.

4 Paragliding
iParaglide: www.iparaglide.com
Learn to be airborne on a tandem
flight with a certified teacher. Coastal
winds ensure breathtaking heights.

5 Rock Climbing
Squamish Rock Guides: 604 892
7816; www.squamishrockguides.com
Squamish is one of the top climbing
areas in North America. You'll have to
be brave to tackle Stawamus Chief, a
formidable cliff rising 2,139 ft (652 m).

6 Windsurfing
Squamish Windsports Society:
www.squamishwindsports.com
Windsurfers converge at the mouth of
the Squamish River on Howe Sound.
Squamish Windsports Society
operates the sailing park and rescue
service, and charges a sailing fee.

7 Diving
Diving Locker: 604 736 2681;
www.divinglocker.ca
Find marine life, diving spots, and
artificial reefs at Howe Sound's many
dive sites. The Diving Locker offers
charters, lessons, and equipment.

8 Whitewater Rafting
Fraser River Raft Expeditions:
1 800 363 7238; www.fraserraft.com
Paddle or power raft just two hours
from Vancouver in Yale on the Fraser,
Nahatlatch, and Thompson rivers.
Fraser River Raft Expeditions offer
a choice of rafts and trips.

Rafting on the Fraser River

9 Skydiving
Abbotsford Skydive Center:
604 854 3255; www.vancouver-
skydiving.bc.ca
The view of the Fraser Valley at
3,000 ft (915 m) is amazing. First-
jump tandem lessons are available
from Abbotsford Skydive Center.

10 Glacier Skiing
Whistler Blackcomb: 604 967
8950; www.whistlerblackcomb.com
Horstman Glacier (see p34) offers
128 acres of skiing and incomparable
views year-round.

See map on pp100–103 →

Restaurants

Elegant dining room at Araxi

1 Araxi
MAP F1 ▪ 4222 Village Sq, Whistler ▪ 604 932 4540 ▪ $$$

Local produce is served with a Pacific Northwest slant at this vibrant, classy spot. They have oysters and wild salmon for fish lovers, and lamb confit and steaks for others.

2 Bishop's
MAP B2 ▪ 2183 W 4th Ave ▪ 604 738 2025 ▪ $$$

Chef John Bishop combines intimate dining with flawless service. Seasonal organic ingredients determine the weekly West Coast menu.

3 Workshop Vegetarian Café
MAP E3 ▪ 296 Pemberton Ave, North Vancouver ▪ 604 973 0163 ▪ $

This quirky and cheerful Japanese-inspired café offers many healthy options. Bright and airy, it's great for coffee, cake, or the signature ramen.

4 Salmon House on the Hill
MAP B1 ▪ 2229 Folkstone Way, West Vancouver ▪ 604 926 3212 ▪ $$

Perched in the North Shore hills, this restaurant is known for its green alderwood-grilled BC salmon. Great examples of First Nations art and artifacts complement the rustic yet elegant interior of wood and glass.

5 The Galley Patio & Grill
MAP E4 ▪ 1300 Discovery St ▪ 604 222 1331 ▪ $

With one of the best patios in Vancouver, this beachside restaurant offers good pub-style food and craft beer.

6 Pear Tree
MAP C2 ▪ 4120 E Hastings St, Burnaby ▪ 604 299 2772 ▪ $$

Widely said to be the "Best of the Burbs," the Pear Tree feels world-class. Its menu emphasizes fresh, quality ingredients.

7 La Quercia
MAP B2 ▪ 3689 W 4th Ave ▪ 604 676 1007 ▪ $$

The Vancouverites flock to this restaurant, with an intimate setting, for exceptional Italian dishes, wines, and exemplary service.

8 The Beach House at Dundarave Pier
MAP B1 ▪ 150 25th St, West Vancouver ▪ 604 922 1414 ▪ $$

Sit on the deck of this 1912 house, choose a glass of wine from the long list, and enjoy West Coast cuisine.

9 Trattoria di Umberto
MAP F1 ▪ 4417 Sundial Pl, Whistler ▪ 604 932 5858 ▪ $$$

The warmth of Tuscany is reflected in the imaginative pasta dishes of celebrity chef Umberto Menghi. Other highlights include *cioppino* (Italian fish chowder) and *osso bucco* (braised veal shank). There's a great wine list.

10 Caramba!
MAP F1 ▪ 12–4314 Main St, Town Plaza, Whistler ▪ 604 938 1879 ▪ $$

This relaxed eatery encourages families to share wood-oven pizza, calamari, and rotisserie meats.

Asian Restaurants

1 Ajisai Sushi Bar
MAP B2 ■ 2081 W 42nd Ave
■ 604 266 1428 ■ $$

Tucked within a small shopping center, this authentic Japanese sushi spot is always crowded, but it is worth the wait.

2 Phnom Penh
MAP M4 ■ 244 E Georgia St
■ 604 682 5777 ■ $$

Don't be fooled by the simple decor. Vancouverites line up here for the tasty deep-fried squid and green papaya salad.

3 Maenam
MAP B2 ■ 1938 W 4th Ave ■ 604 730 5579 ■ $$

Enjoy a fine-dining experience at this Thai restaurant with innovative dishes full of flavors.

4 Banana Leaf
MAP B2 ■ 820 W Broadway
■ 604 731 6333 ■ $$

At this classic Malaysian restaurant, start with the appetizer sampler that includes papaya salad, spring rolls, calamari, roti canai, and satay, and then feast on *nasi goreng* (fried rice).

5 Tojo's
MAP B2 ■ 1133 W Broadway
■ 604 872 8050 ■ $$$

Sushi chef Hidekazu Tojo welcomes every guest as warmly as he does the many celebrities who adore his cozy restaurant. Sidle up to the counter

Sushi bar at celebrity spot Tojo's

> **PRICE CATEGORIES**
> For a three-course meal for one with half a bottle of wine (or equivalent meal), taxes and extra charges.
> ....
> $ under $35 $$ $35–85 $$$ over $85

to watch this fascinating showman create delightful concoctions.

6 So Hyang Korean Cuisine
MAP B2 ■ 6345 Fraser St ■ 604 729 0702 ■ $

Enjoy *bibimbap* (rice bowl) and the *kalbi* (barbecued beef short ribs) at this family-owned Korean restaurant. The service is warm and welcoming.

Appetizing green papaya salad

7 Vij's Rangoli
MAP B2 ■ 1480 W 11th Ave ■ 604 736 5711 ■ $

The award-winning dishes here are a West Coast adaptation of various Indian cooking styles. Specialties are curries, marinated lamb, and duck.

8 Ramen Danbo
MAP B2 ■ 1833 W 4th Ave
■ 778 379 8977 ■ $

Enjoy a quick, inexpensive, and delicious meal with hot bowls of broth, filled with traditional Japanese ramen noodles.

9 Sushi Village
MAP F1 ■ 11-4340 Sundial Cres, Whistler ■ 604 932 3330 ■ $$

This place in the heart of Whistler serves the village's best sushi. It's well worth waiting in line for a table (no reservations for six or less).

10 Chau Veggie Express
MAP E4 ■ 5052 Victoria Dr, East Vancouver ■ 604 560 9500 ■ $

This great community veggie/vegan restaurant serves healthy Vietnamese food, and has excellent service.

See map on p100–101

Streetsmart

Items on display at an
antiques shop in Gastown

Getting To and Around Vancouver and Vancouver Island

Arriving by Air

Vancouver International Airport (YVR) is located in Richmond, 9 miles (14.5 km) from downtown Vancouver. It has two terminals – the Main Terminal for international and domestic flights, and the South Terminal for small aircrafts. The cheapest and quickest way to get to downtown is on the rapid transit Canada Line (a one-time $5 AddFare applies to your journey). Courtesy hotel shuttle pick-up and drop-off areas are at the green canopy outside of Arrivals Level 2 International Terminal and outside the Arrivals Level 1 Domestic Terminal. Car rentals, taxis and public buses also operate from the airport.
Victoria International Airport (YYJ) is 15 miles (24 km) north of Victoria. The airport is serviced by several public buses (No. 70, 72, 83 & 88) and long-distance coaches. The **YYJ Airport Shuttle** departs every 30–60 minutes for major Victoria hotels and there are also taxis and cars for hire.

Arriving by Rail

The main hub for trains is **Pacific Central Station** in downtown Vancouver. **VIA Rail** trains arrive from various destinations all over Canada. The **Amtrak Cascades** route connects Vancouver to Eugene and Portland in Oregon, and to Seattle in Washington with daily trains.

Arriving by Bus

Greyhound buses arrive from the US and other cities in Canada at Pacific Central Station.

Arriving by Car

Vancouver and Victoria airports have a range of car rental company booths. In Vancouver airport they are located on the ground floor of the parking garage and in Victoria airport you will find them in the arrivals hall. Reputable companies include **Avis**, **Hertz**, and **Budget**. Insurance coverage for drivers is mandatory in BC. Check your policy to see if it covers a rental car (some credit cards include car insurance coverage).

Washington state's I-5 connects with Highway 99 at the BC border, leading to Vancouver and Whistler. BC's main Canada–US border crossing is the International Peace Arch in Blaine, Washington.

A good map or GPS navigation device is essential, especially in Vancouver. Highways 1 and 99 can be very busy during rush hour, and there are no freeways bypassing the city core. Speed limits are posted. Right-hand turns on red lights are legal throughout BC unless otherwise posted.

If you are driving in downtown Vancouver, note that a section of Granville Street is closed to private vehicles; signs direct you to side streets.

Arriving by Ferry

BC Ferries connects Vancouver with Victoria, the Gulf Islands, and Nanaimo. Cruise ships dock at Canada Place (see pp14–15). Pleasure boats dock at the many marinas; call **Tourism BC** (see p115) for details.

Traveling by Public Transport

TransLink runs Vancouver's public transit network. To travel you will need a reloadable Compass Card or a Compass Ticket, which covers all transport on the network for a period of 90 minutes. Children under 5 years of age ride free.

Vancouver's SkyTrain is mainly an above-ground light rapid transit system. It includes the Expo Line, Millennium Line, and also the Canada Line, which has 16 stations and links downtown to Vancouver International Airport and Richmond. The SkyTrain system has three fare zones, but on weekdays after 6:30pm, and at the weekend and holidays, it reverts to one zone.

TransLink bus routes extend across much of Greater Vancouver. Bus-only travel is a one-zone fare. Bus drivers do not sell tickets or provide change, so if you don't have a Compass Card or a ticket, pay the exact cash fare when boarding. You will need a Compass Card to switch to the SkyTrain or the SeaBus, which is a catamaran that crosses the harbor in a short 12-minute trip.

Much of Vancouver Island is covered by **BC Transit**. There are two fare zones in Victoria, and children under the age of 5 travel free.

Traveling by Taxi

You can flag down cabs in central Vancouver, but you will need to phone for a taxi in Greater Vancouver and on Vancouver Island. **Bluebird Cabs** are a reputable firm in Victoria.

Traveling by Water taxi

Aquabus and **False Creek Ferries** have various stops around False Creek and Granville Island.

Traveling by Seaplane

Operated by **Harbour Air**, seaplanes cut the journey time between Vancouver and Vancouver Island (Victoria or Nanaimo) down to just 30 minutes. They also run services to Whistler and you can book scenic tours of the area.

Traveling by Bicycle

Vancouver's bike rental scheme **Mobi** is best suited to those who want to ride for 30 minutes or less. If you want to cruise around for the day, or bike on Vancouver Island, hire from one of the many bike rental companies. Try Vancouver's **Spokes Bicycle Rentals** and **Pedaler** in Victoria.

Cyclists must follow the same rules of the road as drivers. Bikes may not be ridden on sidewalks, and wearing a helmet is mandatory. Bikes are allowed on Vancouver's SkyTrain and SeaBus in non-peak hours. Buses in both cities offer bike racks on many routes.

Traveling on Foot

Walking is the best way to explore downtown Vancouver and Victoria, and streets are for the main part very safe. The Seawall *(see p12)* is a fantastic walking path around Stanley Park and on toward False Creek Inlet. In Victoria, the Inner Harbour promenade has views of historic buildings and the harbor *(see p28)*.

DIRECTORY

ARRIVING BY AIR

Vancouver International Airport (YVR)
604 207 7077
yvr.ca

Victoria International Airport (YYJ)
250 953 7500
victoriaairport.com

YYJ Airport Shuttle
yyjairportshuttle.com

ARRIVING BY RAIL

Amtrak Cascades
1 800 872 7245
amtrakcascades.com

Pacific Central Station
MAP M5 ■ 1150 Station St 888-842-7245

VIA Rail
1 888 842 7245
viarail.ca

ARRIVING BY BUS

Greyhound
1 800 661 8747
greyhound.ca

ARRIVING BY CAR

Avis
avis.ca

Budget
budget.ca

Hertz
hertz.ca

ARRIVING BY FERRY

BC Ferries
1 888 223 3779
bcferries.com

TRAVELING BY PUBLIC TRANSPORT

BC Transit
250 382 6161
bctransit.com

TransLink
604 953 3333
translink.ca

TRAVELING BY TAXI

Bluebird Cabs
250 382 2222
taxicab.com

TRAVELING BY WATERTAXI

Aquabus
604 689 5858
theaquabus.com

False Creek Ferries
604 684 7781
granvilleislandferries.bc.ca

TRAVELING BY SEAPLANE

Harbour Air
1 800 665 0212
harbourair.com

TRAVELING BY BICYCLE

Mobi
778 655 1800
mobibikes.ca

Pedaler
778 265 7433
thepedaler.ca

Spokes Bicycle Rentals
604 688 5141
spokesbicyclerentals.com

Practical Information

Passports and Visas

A valid passport, with a visa when needed, must be presented by visitors upon entry to Canada. Residents of many countries, such as Australia, New Zealand, the US, and the majority of European countries (including the UK) do not need a visa, but they do require an online Electronic Travel Authorization (eTA) to fly to or even transit through Canada. Visitors may remain in Canada for up to six months. The website of the government's **Global Affairs Canada** department has further detailed information on entry regulations.

A number of countries, including the **UK**, **US**, and **Australia**, have consulates in central Vancouver and are able to provide limited consular assistance to their nationals.

Customs and Immigration

The rules governing what can be brought into the country are fairly complex. In general, do not try to bring fresh fruit, vegetables, meat, dairy products, live animals, plants, or firearms into Canada without obtaining authorization in advance. Limited amounts of alcohol and tobacco may be imported into the country duty-free by visitors who are of age (19 and 18 years old, respectively). Upon entry into Canada, all visitors must declare any cash amount equal to or more than C$10,000.

Travel Safety Advice

Visitors can get up-to-date travel safety information from the **UK Foreign and Commonwealth Office**, the **US Department of State**, and the **Australian Department of Foreign Affairs and Trade**.

Travel Insurance

Buy comprehensive travel insurance in advance, and check that it covers theft, loss, and cancellation of travel plans. Unless your health insurance covers medical costs while traveling, buying comprehensive health and dental insurance is also highly recommended: Canada does not offer free medical services to visitors.

Health

No vaccinations are necessary to visit Canada, but there are dangers associated with wilderness expeditions to the backcountry. Seek local advice about wild animals (including cougars and bears), dangerous plants (including poison ivy) and insects (including blackflies and mosquitoes), and always boil water that might be unsafe to drink.

In Vancouver, Victoria, and Whistler, emergency treatment is available 24 hours a day. In rural areas, however, operating hours may vary. Consider going to an urgent care center for minor emergencies: the urgent care center at **UBC Hospital** is open daily from 8am to 10pm. If you do need to visit an emergency room, go to **Vancouver General Hospital**, **Victoria General Hospital**, or, if specialist emergency treatment for children is required, **BC Children's Hospital**.

For confidential health information and advice, call **HealthLink BC**.

Personal Security

Most visits to Vancouver and Vancouver Island are trouble free, although there are some common-sense precautions to take. Keep valuables in the room or hotel safe, along with a separate copy of your credit card numbers and their helpline numbers in case of theft or loss. Leave nothing visible in your vehicle and take all valuables with you, including documents.

The Entertainment District downtown can be the scene of rowdy behavior. The Downtown Eastside around Hastings and Main streets, and westward on Hastings from Cambie to Main, is known for drug dealers. Take a bus or taxi to and from Chinatown along Pender Street to avoid this section. Finally, avoid all parks after dark. Crime rates in Victoria are low, though panhandlers may prove a nuisance.

Emergency Services

Various helplines are available to call in a crisis. Call the **emergency number** if you need an ambulance, fire brigade, or urgent police services. If it is not an emergency but you need to speak to the police, telephone the **Vancouver Police** or the **Victoria Police**, depending on your location.

Travelers with Specific Needs

Travelers with mobility, sensory and/or cognitive disabilities will find towns and cities in Vancouver and Vancouver Island very accessible. All public buildings are required to have wheelchair access and provide suitable toilet facilities, and almost all street corners will have dropped kerbs. Car rental companies can provide vehicles with hand controls at no extra charge, but you will need to book ahead. Public transport is universally accessible and passengers with reduced mobility may be entitled to priority boarding and free travel for one companion. For details, check the website of the **CTA** (Canadian Transportation Agency). Provincial tourist offices are the top source of information on accessible hotels, motels, and sights. You can find further information for travelers with specific needs in Canada on the **Access to Travel** website.

Currency and Banking

The unit of currency is the Canadian dollar (CAD or C$), divided into 100 cents. Banknotes (bills) come in denominations of $5, $10, $20, $50, and $100, while coins are 5, 10, and 25 cents, and $1 (locally known as a "loonie") and $2 (locally known as a "toonie"). Plan to arrive with at least $100 in local currency and get change for tipping and travel (without a Compass Card, you'll need exact change for buses).

Telephone and Internet

If you have an unlocked mobile phone that operates on the GSM bands, you can purchase a SIM card for local networks on a pay-as-you-go basis. Free Wi-Fi is available in most bars, restaurants, and public libraries.

Public pay phones are rare, but if you do manage to find one, it will usually be both coin- and card-operated, charging 50 cents to $1 for a local call.

Local telephone numbers are prefixed by area code 604. For a long-distance number in North America, dial the prefix 1 and then the area number. To dial abroad, dial 011 + country code + city code (dropping the first 0).

DIRECTORY

PASSPORTS AND VISAS

Australian Consulate
604 694 6160
canada.embassy.gov.au

Global Affairs Canada
international.gc.ca

UK Consulate General
604 683 4421
ukincanada.fco.gov.uk

US Consulate General
604 685 4311
ca.usembassy.gov

TRAVEL SAFETY ADVICE

Australian Department of Foreign Affairs and Trade
dfat.gov.au
smartraveller.gov.au

UK Foreign and Commonwealth Office
gov.uk/foreign-travel-advice

US Department of State
state.gov/travel

HEALTH

BC Children's Hospital
MAP E4 ■ 4480 Oak St, Vancouver
604 875 2345

HealthLink BC
811

UBC Hospital
MAP E4 ■ 2211 Wesbrook Mall, Vancouver
604 822 7121

Vancouver General Hospital
MAP E4 ■ 899 W 12th Ave, Vancouver
604 875 4111

Victoria General Hospital
MAP E6 ■ 1 Hospital Way, Victoria
250 727 4212

EMERGENCY SERVICES

Emergency Number
911

Vancouver Police
MAP L3 ■ 2120 Cambie St
604 717 3321

Victoria Police
MAP Q1 ■ 850 Caledonia Ave
250 995 7654

TRAVELERS WITH SPECIFIC NEEDS

Access to Travel
accesstotravel.gc.ca

CTA
canada.ca

Postal Services

Post offices and service counters in Vancouver and on Vancouver Island are operated by **Canada Post**. Check its website to find the nearest outlet. Current costs for letters and postcards up to 30g are 85 cents nationally, $1.20 to the US, and $2.50 for international mail.

Television and Radio

Canada's most popular TV stations are **CBC**, **CTV**, **Global**, and, in BC, the **Knowledge Network**. Popular radio stations include **CBC Radio Two** (FM 105.7) for classical music, **CFOX** (FM 99.3) for rock music, **NEWS 1130** (AM 1130) for news, and **QMFM** (FM 103.5) for easy-listening music.

Newspapers and Magazines

The *Vancouver Sun* and *The Province*, BC's two largest newspapers, are produced in Vancouver. The two national newspapers, *The Globe and Mail* and the *National Post*, are also available. *The Georgia Straight*, a weekly Vancouver tabloid, is available free at cafés, bars, bookshops, libraries, and street boxes, and is the best for local music and art listings.

Opening Hours

Most shops are open from 10am to 6pm Monday to Saturday (often later on Thursday). Department stores and shops in malls and retail districts may stay open to 9pm Monday to Saturday, and open on Sunday from 11am or noon to 5pm. Many shops close on January 1, July 1, Labor Day, Thanksgiving, and December 25.

Time Difference

Vancouver and Vancouver Island are on Pacific Time (eight hours behind GMT). Daylight Saving Time begins in mid-March when clocks are turned forward one hour, and ends in early November when clocks are turned back one hour.

Electrical Appliances

Canada uses a 110-volt, 60-cycle electrical system. Electrical sockets accept plugs with two or three flat pins. Visitors will need a plug adapter and voltage converter for all appliances that were not manufactured in North America.

Weather

The temperate coastal climate of Vancouver and Vancouver Island is at its best April to November. Rain falls intermittently November to March, but low season is a good time for storm-watching.

In the city and along the coast, winter temperatures rarely drop below freezing, but are far lower high up in the mountains. Whistler sees an annual snowfall of 39 ft (11.9 m).

Visitor Information

Tourism Vancouver *(see p15)*, **Tourism Victoria**, **Vancouver Island Travel**, and **Tourism BC** all have tourist information centers across the region as well as websites that have plenty of useful resources for travelers.

Trips and Tours

Walking tours are a great way to discover the area. Take a walk with **Tours by Locals** or learn about Vancouver's Chinatown with tour guides from the **Chinese Cultural Centre** *(see p40)*. **Forbidden Vancouver** offers tours about the Prohibition and the darker side of the city's history, while **Discover the Past** brings alive Victoria's history.

Pacific Coach Lines runs various day trips, including a tour of Victoria and Butchart Gardens en route to Vancouver. **West Coast Sightseeing** has a daily shuttle from Vancouver to Whistler and operates a year-round city bus tour. The **Vancouver Trolley Company** also operates a hop-on-hop-off service.

To view orcas, Dall's porpoises, seals, and other wildlife, take a trip with **Wild Whales**, which departs from Granville Island for the Gulf of Georgia and beyond. **Vancouver Whale Watch** has Zodiac-style boats with onboard naturalists. **Steveston SeaBreeze Adventures** runs larger vessels from the Fraser River to the Gulf Islands. Coast Salish guides from **Takaya Tours** lead two-hour paddling trips in a 12-passenger, traditional-style, oceangoing canoe.

Shopping

Vancouver has an excellent selection of shops *(see pp60–61)*. In Victoria, you can spend hours browsing independent boutiques, such as the one-of-a kind shops in Market Square, set in pretty heritage buildings. Vancouver Island is a great place to visit galleries exhibiting First Nations art.

Taxes are not included in the listed price, so when making a purchase add a further 7 per cent for PST (Provincial Sales Tax) and 5 per cent for GST (Goods and Services Tax) on most items.

Dining

There is a great range of restaurants and cafés in Vancouver and on Vancouver Island (see pp58–9). Street food, such as dim sum, pulled pork sandwiches, and tacos, is available from food trucks in Vancouver; download the **Street Food App** to find where the best trucks are parked.

It's also easy to find good-quality, good-value Asian food in Vancouver, Victoria, and Richmond, and local producers sell at the **Granville Island Public Market** (see pp24–5).

Service charges and tips are not usually added to bills, although they may be if your party consists of six people or more. Plan on tipping approximately 15 percent of your total bill's pre-tax amount.

Accommodation

There are many excellent hotels in the Vancouver area (see pp116–19). For budget or more unusual options, check the websites of **Backpackers Hostels Canada, Parks Canada Reservation Service**, or **BC Guest Ranchers Association**. Peak rates apply April–December. In BC, accommodation is taxed with 8 percent provincial hotel room tax. Some properties are also required to add an additional 3 percent tourism tax on hotel rooms (this applies in Victoria, Whistler, Tofino, Ucluelet, and Vancouver).

DIRECTORY

POSTAL SERVICES

Canada Post
w canadapost.ca

TELEVISION AND RADIO

CBC
w cbc.ca

CBC Radio Two
w cbcmusic.ca/radio2

CFOX
w cfox.com

CTV
w ctv.ca

Global
w globaltv.com

Knowledge Network
w knowledge.ca

NEWS 1130
w news1130.com

QMFM
w iheartradio.ca/qmfm

NEWSPAPERS AND MAGAZINES

National Post
w nationalpost.com

The Georgia Straight
w straight.com

The Globe and Mail
w theglobeandmail.com

The Province
w theprovince.com

Vancouver Sun
w vancouversun.com

VISITOR INFORMATION

Tourism BC
w hellobc.com

Tourism Victoria
w tourismvictoria.com

Vancouver Island Travel
w vancouverisland.travel

TRIPS AND TOURS

Discover the Past
w discoverthepast.com

Forbidden Vancouver
w forbiddenvancouver.ca

Pacific Coach Lines
w pacificcoach.com

Steveston SeaBreeze Adventures
w seabreezeadventures.ca

Takaya Tours
w takayatours.com

Tours by Locals
w toursbylocals.com

Vancouver Trolley Company
w vancouvertrolley.com

Vancouver Whale Watch
w vancouverwhalewatch.com

West Coast Sightseeing
w westcoastsightseeing.com

Wild Whales
w whalesvancouver.com

DINING

Street Food App
w streetfoodapp.com/vancouver

ACCOMMODATION

Backpackers Hostels Canada
w backpackers.ca

BC Guest Ranchers Association
w bcguestranches.com

Parks Canada Reservation Service
w reservation.pc.gc.ca

Places to Stay

Vancouver Luxury and Boutique Hotels

The Listel Hotel
MAP J3 ■ 1300 Robson St ■ 604 684 8461 ■ www.thelistelhotel.com ■ $$$
A beautiful boutique hotel with rooms that are all filled with art by local artists. There are two eateries on-site: Forage, for fresh and innovative cooking, and Timber, for comfort food and craft beers.

Metropolitan Hotel
MAP K3 ■ 645 Howe St ■ 604 687 1122 ■ www.metropolitan.com ■ $$$
Every step is taken to maximize the comfort of guests here, with European down duvets, marble bathrooms, an indoor pool, and a health club. There is also a business center on-site.

Opus Hotel
MAP J5 ■ 322 Davie St ■ 604 642 6787 ■ www.vancouver.opushotel.com ■ $$$
This stylish boutique hotel is a Yaletown trendsetter. Take advantage of the on-site Italian restaurant and relax in the sophisticated lounge.

Rosewood Hotel Georgia
MAP K3 ■ 801 W Georgia St ■ 604 682 5566 ■ www.rosewoodhotels.com ■ $$$
Treat yourself to a stay at this elegant and legendary retreat. It first opened as the Hotel Georgia in 1927, and has been beautifully restored. The spa and Hawksworth restaurant are exemplary. Head to Prohibition, the chic bar in the basement, for innovative cocktails.

St. Regis Hotel
MAP K3 ■ 602 Dunsmuir St ■ 604 681 1135 ■ www.stregishotel.com ■ $$$
In an ideal location for shopping and clubbing, the St. Regis offers rooms with balconies, oversized tubs, and stellar views of the harbor, city, and mountains. Breakfast is complimentary.

Shangri-La Hotel
MAP J3 ■ 1128 W Georgia St ■ 604 689 1120 ■ www.shangri-la.com ■ $$$
In the heart of downtown, this sumptuous hotel offers 119 luxury rooms. The oversized bathrooms even have TVs embedded in the mirrors. Many of the rooms have balconies.

Wedgewood Hotel & Spa
MAP J3 ■ 845 Hornby St ■ 604 689 7777 ■ www.wedgewoodhotel.com ■ $$$
Founded by hotelier Eleni Skalbania, this boutique hotel has European flair. The place caters to those who prefer their accommodation upscale, verging on exclusive. Maid service twice daily says it all.

Westin Bayshore
MAP J2 ■ 1601 Bayshore Drive ■ 604 682 3377 ■ www.westinbayshore.com ■ $$$
Sitting on Coal Harbour, between Stanley Park and downtown, this hotel offers guests the best of both worlds: nature and outdoor activities plus close proximity to the downtown hustle and bustle, with comfortable rooms to retreat to after a busy day.

Vancouver Business and Suite Hotels

Best Western Plus Chateau Granville
MAP J4 ■ 1100 Granville St ■ 604 669 7070 ■ www.chateaugranville.com ■ $$
A frequent choice for out-of-towners seeking a good location and value for money, this 15-story hotel offers mainly one-bedroom suites, but has some smaller, standard rooms as well. Suites come with microwaves.

Residence Inn Vancouver Downtown
MAP J4 ■ 1234 Hornby St ■ 604 688 1234 ■ www.marriott.com ■ $$
Close to Yaletown and the Davie Street shopping area, this hotel's spacious suites with kitchens and seating areas are a great option for an extended stay. There is an indoor pool, a gym, and complimentary breakfast.

Sunset Inn and Suites
MAP H4 ■ 1111 Burnaby St ■ 604 688 2474 ■ www.sunsetinn.com ■ $$
Found in a high-rise in the West End, this hotel's

location is central but off the main thoroughfare, so it is quieter than some others. It is suitable for short- and long-term stays, and breakfast and parking area are available.

Fairmont Waterfront

MAP K2 ▪ 900 Canada Pl ▪ 604 691 1991 ▪ www.fairmont.com ▪ $$$

Linked to the convention center by an enclosed walkway, this harborside property has an accessible rooftop garden, a 24-hour gym, an outdoor heated pool, and a stylish cocktail bar. Stay on the Fairmont Gold levels to enjoy additional service and amenities.

Four Seasons Hotel, Vancouver

MAP K3 ▪ 791 W Georgia St ▪ 604 609 9333 ▪ www.fourseasons.com ▪ $$$

Set in the ideal business location, centrally situated above the Pacific Centre Mall, this hotel goes the extra mile, with a 24-hour concierge, a health club, indoor and outdoor pools, an elegant lounge and restaurant, meeting-room facilities, 24-hour room service, and valet parking.

Georgian Court Hotel

MAP L4 ▪ 773 Beatty St ▪ 604 682 5555 ▪ www.georgiancourt.com ▪ $$$

Providing a great location for sports fans in town to take in a game (BC Place Stadium and Rogers Arena are mere minutes away), this well-appointed business and leisure hotel offers air-conditioned rooms and suites, plus a 24-hour fitness center. Enjoy the on-site Italian kitchen and bar.

Pan Pacific Vancouver

MAP L2 ▪ 300-999 Canada Place ▪ 604 662 8111 ▪ www.panpacific.com ▪ $$$

Soaring over the famous waterfront, the Pan's rooms and luxury suites provide spectacular views of the North Shore mountains. With the convention center located in the same complex, this place is generally regarded as North America's premiere convention hotel.

Vancouver Mid-Priced Hotels

Blue Horizon Hotel

MAP J3 ▪ 1225 Robson St ▪ 604 688 1411 ▪ www.bluehorizonhotel.com ▪ $$

Gorgeous views abound in this contemporary hotel, as each room has wrap-around windows and a balcony. Other facilities in each room include a fridge, a coffee maker, and air-conditioning.

Century Plaza Hotel & Spa

MAP J4 ▪ 1015 Burrard St ▪ 604 687 0575 ▪ www.century-plaza.com ▪ $$

This hotel is a modest, good-value choice. The really big draw here is the European-style spa (see p49), which has a large indoor pool and steam room as well as many excellent treatments. There's also a convenient lounge and restaurant, and a cappuccino bar.

Moda Hotel

MAP K4 ▪ 900 Seymour St ▪ 604 683 4251 ▪ www.modahotel.ca ▪ $$

A good-value, boutique hotel in a heritage 1908 building that blends

old-world style with contemporary interiors. There is a choice of an Italian restaurant, cocktail bar and a sports bar on-site.

Skwachàys Lodge

MAP L4 ▪ 29/31 W Pender ▪ 604 687 3589 ▪ www.skwachays.com ▪ $$

An Aboriginal-owned boutique hotel and art gallery with individually decorated rooms and a floor dedicated to offering subsidized housing for indigenous artists. The Downtown Eastside location is on the edge of a rougher neighbourhood, so consider a taxi at night.

Sylvia Hotel

MAP G2 ▪ 1154 Gilford St ▪ 604 681 9321 ▪ www.sylviahotel.com ▪ $$

The West End's grande dame is a favorite for its relaxed yet sophisticated atmosphere and a really fabulous location right on English Bay. Some rooms are tiny, but the big draws are the lounge and restaurant overlooking the water. It's a pet-friendly hotel, and covered paid parking is available.

Granville Island Hotel

MAP H6 ▪ 1253 Johnston St ▪ 604 683 7373 ▪ www.granvilleislandhotel.com ▪ $$$

With delightful rooms overlooking False Creek, this intimate hotel, located right on Granville Island, features pretty wooden shutters, beamed ceilings, and sumptuous oversized bath tubs. Dine at the refined Dockside restaurant, or choose from the many excellent nearby eateries.

Vancouver B&Bs and Guesthouses

Barclay House B&B
MAP H3 ▪ 1351 Barclay St ▪ 604 605 1351 ▪ www. barclayhouse.com ▪ $$
A perennial West End favorite, this classic 1904 home features spacious two-room suites, attentive staff, a full three-course breakfast, cookies on arrival, in-room refrigerator and drinks, and free parking.

Corkscrew Inn B&B
MAP E4 ▪ 2735 W 2nd Ave ▪ 604 733 7276 ▪ www. corkscrewinn.com ▪ $$
In a lovely restored 1912 Craftsman-style house, this funky Kitsilano B&B combines Art Deco charm – including dozens of stained-glass windows – with upscale amenities. Soom rooms have fireplaces and private balconies. Take a peek at the curios in the small on-site wine museum.

English Bay Inn
MAP G2 ▪ 1968 Comox St ▪ 604 683 8002 ▪ www. englishbayinn.com ▪ $$
A West End hideaway with cozy antique furniture and air-conditioned en suite rooms. The full breakfast by the fireplace is a pleasant start to the day.

O Canada House
MAP J3 ▪ 1114 Barclay St ▪ 604 688 0555 ▪ www. ocanadahouse.com ▪ $$
Built in 1897, this lovely guesthouse reflects the early elegance of the West End, including a parlor with a fireplace. A gourmet breakfast, evening sherry, 24-hour pantry for guests, and free parking is available.

Victorian Hotel
MAP L3 ▪ 514 Homer St ▪ 604 681 6369 ▪ www. victorianhotel.ca ▪ $$
Built in 1898 as one of the city's first guest-houses, this hotel has been very carefully restored to retain its Victorian-era ambience, with bay windows, high ceilings, antique furnishings, and hardwood floors. A comfortable setting, with beautiful bathrooms and down duvets on the beds.

West End Guest House
MAP J3 ▪ 1362 Haro St ▪ 604 681 2889 ▪ www. westendguesthouse.com ▪ $$
This pretty pink and grey 1906 Victorian inn in Stanley Park offers one- and two-bedroom suites. There is free parking and bike storage, and full hot breakfast is served daily.

Vancouver Budget Hotels

Buchan Hotel
MAP H2 ▪ 1906 Haro St ▪ 604 685 5354 ▪ www. buchanhotel.com ▪ $
This 1920s, three-story property offers good value for money with its vintage European-style, no-frills accommodation and its location; you'd be hard-pressed to sleep closer to Stanley Park. The communal lounge with a fireplace is a bonus.

Hostelling International Vancouver Downtown
MAP H4 ▪ 1114 Burnaby St ▪ 604 684 4565 ▪ www. hihostels.ca ▪ $
Shared and private rooms are offered in this friendly West End spot. There's free breakfast, and the shared kitchen can help with the other meals. Guests can relax on the lovely, sunny rooftop patio.

University of British Columbia
MAP A2 ▪ 5961 Student Union Blvd ▪ 604 822 1001 ▪ www.suitesatubc. com ▪ $
From May to August, take your pick from 3,000 rooms on UBC's beautiful campus. Year-round, one-bedroom suites with kitchens are available. Each is spotlessly kept and offers free Wi-Fi. UBC is a city in itself, with many amenities on its grounds and nearby.

YWCA Hotel
MAP K5 ▪ 733 Beatty St ▪ 604 895 5830 ▪ www. ywcavan.org/hotel ▪ $
This is a secure, 12-story downtown high-rise with air-conditioned rooms to suit all types of travelers, including families. It has TVs in many of the rooms and is a great place for those who need their gym fix, with free admission to the fitness center. The hotel is also fully wheelchair accessible.

Kingston Hotel
MAP K4 ▪ 757 Richards St ▪ 604 684 9024 ▪ www. kingstonhotelvancouver. com ▪ $$
Set in a relaxed 1910 heritage building, this hotel has private and shared baths, day and overnight storage, a TV lounge, sauna, and a good pub. The room rate includes an excellent continental breakfast. Guests can also relax by the fireplace in the lounge.

Vancouver Island Hotels

Ocean Island Backpackers Inn, Victoria

MAP Q2 ■ 791 Pandora Ave ■ 250 385 1789 ■ www.oceanisland.com ■ $

Clean and comfortable, this hostel is in a historic building near Victoria's Inner Harbour. Dorms and private rooms are available. Breakfasts and dinners are included.

Paul's Motor Inn, Victoria

MAP E6 ■ 1900 Douglas St ■ 250 382 9231 ■ www.paulsmotorinn.com ■ $

Centrally located in a safe area, Paul's is a great budget base with on-site parking from which to enjoy downtown Victoria. Rooms have mini-fridges and are pet friendly.

Chateau Victoria Hotel & Suites, Victoria

MAP Q3 ■ 740 Burdett Ave ■ 250 382 4221 ■ www.chateauvictoria.com ■ $$

Located steps away from Victoria's Inner Harbour, this four-star business and leisure hotel features Victoria's only rooftop restaurant and lounge on the 18th floor.

Coast Bastion Hotel, Nanaimo

MAP D4 ■ 11 Bastion St ■ 250 753 6601 ■ www.coasthotels.com ■ $$

The best of Nanaimo's accommodation offerings, this smart hotel has great views across the waterfront. There's a business center, a great restaurant, a fitness room and a spa.

Delta Victoria Ocean Pointe Resort, Victoria

MAP N2 ■ 100 Harbour Rd ■ 250 360 2999 ■ www.marriott.com ■ $$

This harborfront hotel offers modern, quiet, and air-conditioned rooms. The amenities include an indoor pool, 24-hour gym, and sports courts.

Heathergate House, Victoria

MAP E6 ■ 122 Simcoe St ■ 250 383 0068 ■ www.victoria-vacationrentals.com ■ $$

This hotel is located in a near-perfect spot in a quiet area near Victoria's busy Inner Harbour. The plush suites all have a private bath and kitchenette, and there is also a well-appointed garden cottage that easily sleeps four. Full English breakfast is included in the price of the rooms.

Huntingdon Manor Hotel, Victoria

MAP N4 ■ 330 Quebec St ■ 250 381 3456 ■ www.huntingdonmanor.com ■ $$

This affordable hotel, right by the Inner Harbour, offers a range of cozy rooms and stylish suites, including family suites for up to six people. The breakfast is included in the room rate.

Inn at Laurel Point, Victoria

MAP N3 ■ 680 Montreal St ■ 250 386 8721 ■ www.laurelpoint.com ■ $$

The spacious rooms here come with a view of Victoria's Inner Harbour. The Sunday buffet-style brunch in the Aura Restaurant is excellent.

Magnolia Hotel & Spa, Victoria

MAP P3 ■ 623 Courtney St ■ 250 381 0999 ■ www.magnoliahotel.com ■ $$

This award-winning hotel wins over guests with its unbeatable location and service. The sumptuous rooms feature four-poster beds and marble bathrooms with deep soaker tubs.

Fairmont Empress Hotel, Victoria

MAP P4 ■ 721 Government St ■ 250 384 8111 ■ www.fairmont.com ■ $$$

The most famous hotel on the West Coast, Victoria's top luxury hotel offers small but elegant rooms. Make a reservation to take English-style tea in the glorious lobby (see p99), a pricey but note-worthy experience.

Oak Bay Beach Hotel, Victoria

MAP E6 ■ 1175 Beach Dr ■ 250 598 4556 ■ www.oakbaybeachhotel.com ■ $$$

The rooms at this hotel are elegant and feature large spa-like bathrooms, patios, and fireplaces. Guests can soak in the seaside mineral baths, or enjoy a drink at the pub.

Wickaninnish Inn, Tofino

MAP A4 ■ 500 Osprey Ln, Tofino ■ 250 725 3100 ■ www.wickinn.com ■ $$$

Perched dramatically on a rocky shelf overlooking Chesterman Beach, this highly acclaimed inn offers luxurious lodgings done in a modern West Coast style. With a great spa and gourmet restaurant, it's the perfect getaway spot.

For a key to hotel price categories see p116

General Index

Acknowledgments

Author
Constance Brissenden is along time BC resident living in downtown Vancouver. She has written numerous travel, history, and children's books, and is co-author of the Dorling Kindersley *Eyewitness Travel Guide to the Pacific Northwest*.

Additional contributor
Rachel Mills

Publishing Director Georgina Dee

Publisher Vivien Antwi

Design Director Phil Ormerod

Editorial Sophie Adam, Ankita Awasthi Tröger, Dipika Dasgupta, Rachel Fox, Alison McGill, Sally Schafer, Hollie Teague, Danielle Watt

Design Tessa Bindloss, Priyanka Thakur, Vinita Venugopal

Commissioned Photography Gunter Marx, Alvin Kanak

Picture Research Taiyaba Khatoon; Susie Peachey, Ellen Root; Rituraj Singh

Cartography Mohammad Hassan, Suresh Kumar, James Macdonald

DTP Jason Little

Production Igrain Roberts

Factchecker Lisa Voormeij

Proofreader Susanne Hillen

Indexer Helen Peters

First edition produced by International Book Productions Inc., Toronto

Picture Credits
The publisher would like to thank the following for their kind permission to reproduce their photographs:
Key: a-above; b-below/bottom; c-centre; f-far; l-left; r-right; t-top

123RF.com: pngstudio 11cb; ronniechua 13tr.

Alamy Stock Photo: age fotostock 56t; All Canada Photos 3tl, 66–7, 105tl; Amazing Images 4t; Mieneke Andeweg-van Rijn 15crb; Aurora Photos 33tr; B.O'Kane 60tl; Brett Baunton 95cla; Tibor Bognar 62tl; David Buzzard 35bl; Chris Cheadle 35tl, 48bl, 98tl; Engel Ching 22–3; Felix Choo 98br; Christian Kober 1 75tr; Shaun Cunningham 94tl; Danita Delimont 18clb; Keith Douglas 50bl; 90–91; Elena Elisseeva 46–7; Dan Galic 102br; GerryRousseau 100tl; David Gowans 96tr; HI / Gunter Marx 102t; Dave G. Houser 6br, 11cra; imageBROKER 61br; Images by Morgana 42t; Incite Photography 10bl, 18br; Maria Janicki 86ca; JTB Media Creation; Inc. 4crb; Brenda Kean 13crb; John Keates 32br; Jason Kwan 17crb; Douglas Lander 17tl, 84cr; Roy Langstaff 52clb; Edmund Lowe 99cla; Martin Thomas Photography 57cb; Gunter Marx 34clb; McCanner 105crb; Andrew Melbourne 51br; John Mitchell 71cl; Nikreates 20bl, 42bc, 70b; Overflightstock Ltd 32–3; Paul Thompson Images 38cb; pbpvision 1; David Pearson 55clb; Kim Petersen 50t; Prisma by Dukas Presseagentur GmbH 31bl; RM USA 57tr; Rolf Hicker Photography 93t; David Wei 20cr; Michael Wheatley 11cr, 14crb, 18–19, 26–7, 27cb, 30bl, 31tr, 51clb, 63tr, 70tr, 76cla, 80cla; Xinhua 41br; 87tl; ZUMA Press; Inc. 54bl.

Art Gallery of Greater Victoria: The Thomas Gardiner Keir Bequest. 29cra.

AWL Images: Walter Bibikow 3tr, 108–9; ImageBROKER 4clb, 10cla, 83tl; Stefano Politi Markovina 12br; 53b, 61tr.

BC Sports Hall of Fame and Museum: 77tl.

Chambar: Luis Valdizon 58cb.

Dockside Restaurant and Brewing Company: 88tl.

Dreamstime.com: Steve Boyko 62b; Dan Breckwoldt 104b; Brenda Carson 29tl; Engel Ching 44b; Robert Cocquyt 96bl; Carrie Cole 44tr; Jerry Coli 24cla; Deymos 25tl, 61cl, 86br; Edonalds 7tr; Alexandre Fagundes De Fagundes 19tc; Fallsview 4cla; Sebastien Fremont 101t; Lucas Inacio 84–5; Jpldesigns 69br; Mariusz Jurgielewicz 17cb; Katyenka 33crb; Volodymyr Kyrylyuk 64bl; Erik Lattwein 2tr, 14bl, 36–7, 68cla; Pierre Leclerc 15tl; Ian Mcdonald 10clb; Meunierd 43tr; minnystock 24–5, 28cra, 28–9b; Borirak Mongkolget 107ca; Denis Pepin 94–5; Gino Rigucci 6cla; Ronniechua 10c; Paul Sahota 92cla; Jean-jacques Serol 41c; Brandon Smith 4cr; Nalidsa Sukprasert 45tr; Vof Vermeulen Perdaen & Steyaert 74tr; Zhenwang Wang 47cr, 101br; Bill Warchol 103cl; Alfred Wekelo 49tr; Gene Zhang 14–15.

Fairmont Pacific Rim: Paul Warchol 49cl.

Four Seasons Hotel Vancouver: Yew Bar 79cr.

Four Seasons Resort Whistler: 48t.

Getty Images: Barrett & MacKay 76br; Andrew Chin 53tr, 56bl, 65br; Jim Corwin 39clb; Richard Cummins 63cl, 82cla; Design Pics / Emily Riddell 16cr; Bertil Ericson 39tr; JTB Photo 16bl; Christopher Morris 83crb; Stock Montage 38tr; Jeff Vinnick 47tl; Michael Wheatley 30ca, 45cl.

Granville Island Brewing: 25c.